A
Geologist's View
of
Cape Cod

A Geologist's View Of Cape Cod
was originally published under
The Natural History Press Imprint

Arthur N. Strahler

A
Geologist's View
of
Cape Cod

PARNASSUS IMPRINTS
Box 335
Orleans, Massachusetts 02653

Published by arrangement with Doubleday,
A division of Bantam, Doubleday, Dell
Publishing Group, Inc.

Library of Congress Catalog Card Number 66–24306

ISBN 0-940160-39-0

Paranassus Imprints edition published May, 1988.

Contents

LIST OF ILLUSTRATIONS

A
Geologist's View
of
Cape Cod

1. The outline of Cape Cod. The area shown spans about forty miles from west to east.

Introduction

To a geologist, Cape Cod shows an intriguing map outline—one
that raises many questions. As all visitors who come here know,
Cape Cod has the outline of a bent arm—something like that of a
boy flexing his arm to show his strength—except that the biceps
muscle is disappointingly shrunken and the fist is a bit too small
(Figure 1). The Cape extends about twenty-five miles eastward
from the mainland of Massachusetts, then about thirty miles north
and northwest to Race Point, its most northerly point. Nowhere
is the Cape more than ten miles wide. Through its whole extent,
Cape Cod consists almost entirely of sand, gravel, silt, clay, and
boulders, with no solid bedrock whatsoever showing anywhere or
even to be found at depths of many feet below the surface. All of
this material was brought here by great ice sheets during the Ice
Age, which has only just ended, geologically speaking.

To the geologist this great deposit of glacial material is a very young feature, as landscapes of North America go. The more he studies the Cape, the more the geologist can find of interest in the delightful variety of beaches, bays, cliffs, dunes, hills, plains, and lakes which attract so many thousands of people and cause them to return each summer. He can see here the work of the great glaciers of ice as they shaped the first outlines of the Cape and also the forms fashioned by waves, wind, and streams which have worked unceasingly since the ice sheets wasted away.

In this book you will read the geologist's story of Cape Cod from the Ice Age to the present. As you do so, you will learn much about the processes of geology which create landscape features. The basic ideas given here can be applied to many other regions as well, so that the Cape can serve as a splendid summer laboratory of the earth sciences. As you travel from beach to pond in the Cape Cod National Seashore look for the features which are explained in this book.

How Cape Cod Was Formed

THE CAPE IS VERY YOUNG

Although Cape Cod is a peninsula of New England, it is very unlike the mainland to which it is attached. When we think of New England we have in mind hills and mountains of solid rock—granite and marble, for example. We think of the rock-bound coast of Maine where the waves break on granite many hundreds of millions of years old. We think of the White Mountains of New Hampshire with vast exposures of ancient hard rock in cliffs and bleak, boulder-strewn uplands. Most of New England was already shaped approximately into its present-day landscape long before Cape Cod came into existence. In contrast, Cape Cod is a product of the ice sheets of the *Pleistocene Epoch,* a relatively insignificant fragment of geologic time which began about one million years ago and ended about ten thousand years ago. To any person even ten thousand years is a vast span of time—enough to include easily all of the history of civilization—while one million years of time is almost too much to comprehend. But the rocks of New England were formed from three hundred million to five hundred million years ago and this is a span of time totally beyond anything we as humans can conceive of in terms of the events of our lives.

Actually, Cape Cod was formed rather late in the Pleistocene Epoch, in the final ice-age stage known as the *Wisconsin Stage,* which began some fifty thousand to seventy thousand years ago. During the Wisconsin Stage great ice sheets which originated in the region of Labrador and Hudson Bay made their final invasions into the northeastern United States. Before these ice invasions Cape Cod did not exist; after the last invasion was over the approximate present outlines of Cape Cod, as well as those of Nantucket Island, Marthas Vineyard, and Long Island, were laid out.

BEFORE CAPE COD—WHAT?

If Cape Cod did not exist before the Wisconsin Stage of the Ice Age, what existed instead in this region? As you probably know, the ocean floor close to the eastern coast of the United States is quite shallow for a distance of about one hundred miles out from the coastline. This shallow zone of our continent is known as the *continental shelf.* Rocks much like those of the mainland form the shelf, which can be imagined as a true fringe of the continent submerged under some five hundred feet of water. Before the coming of the ice sheets of the Pleistocene Epoch, part of what is now the shallow continental shelf off New England was above sea level and consisted of a zone of plains and low hills gradually becoming lower toward the east where the former shoreline stood. Geologists call such a region a *coastal plain.* They imagine it to have resembled the present-day coastal plain of New Jersey, Delaware, Maryland, and Virginia, but of course no details of the

New England coastal plain are known because that land surface now lies beneath sea water or is concealed under deposits left by the ice sheets.

SPREADING OF THE ICE SHEETS

During the final, or Wisconsin Stage of the Pleistocene Epoch, starting some fifty thousand to seventy thousand years ago, a great sheet of glacial ice formed over the highlands of Labrador (Figure 2). More snow fell during the winters than could be melted during the summers, so that the snow accumulated in layers, gradually becoming compressed into solid ice. When the ice thickness reached hundreds of feet, the ice began to yield like a thick tar and to spread outward over the ground of surrounding lower areas. As the growth of this great sheet of ice set in, the ice continued to become thicker and thicker, eventually reaching at least ten thousand feet in thickness, spreading as far south as New York City and Long Island and covering all of New England. The ice also spread southward over the low coastal plain where we now find the shallow waters of Cape Cod Bay and the continental shelf east of Cape Cod. We should remember that as the great ice sheets of North America, Europe, and Siberia grew thicker, they held in storage as ice a great deal of ocean water, so that the level of the ocean fell considerably (some geologists estimate as much as three hundred to five hundred feet), and the shoreline of New England must have receded to a line far east of the Cape Cod region. Cape Cod thus came into being as a feature of the mainland, and not as the coastal feature it is today.

WHERE THE ICE SHEETS STOPPED

On the accompanying map of southeastern New England are drawn arrows to show the direction in which the ice moved and the limits which it finally reached (Figure 3). At the farthest extent, the ice of the Wisconsin Stage reached a line running east-

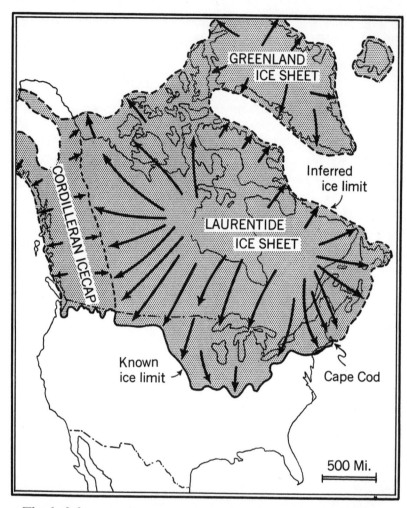

2. The shaded area on this map represents the fullest extent of the ice sheets of the Pleistocene Epoch. Directions of ice flow are shown by heavy arrows. Cape Cod lies at the edge of the ice advance. (Based on data of Professor Richard F. Flint of Yale University.)

ward along Long Island to Montauk Point, through Block Island, then through Marthas Vineyard and Nantucket Island. East of Nantucket the ice margin probably turned northward, but we cannot trace it farther. This chain of islands, like Cape Cod, consists largely of the deposits of sand, gravel, clay, and boulders brought by the ice.

After reaching its line of farthest advance, and holding that position for thousands of years, the ice margin began to recede northward, because the rate of melting and evaporation of the ice was for a time more rapid than could be equaled by new ice spreading southward. Thus the ice margin came to occupy a second line, as shown on the map. This line ran along the north shore of Long Island, through Fishers Island and along the south shore of Rhode Island, then through the Elizabeth Islands and along the east side of Buzzards Bay. About where the Cape Cod Canal is located today, the ice margin bent sharply east to run along the north side of Cape Cod close to the south shore of Cape Cod Bay. The ice margin took a sharp jog north along the forearm of the Cape, then ran southeastward out to sea, probably eventually turning north.

The second position of the ice margin, just described, was held for a long period of time—perhaps several thousands of years— during which time the rate at which the ice was spreading south just balanced the rate at which the ice was being lost by melting and evaporation at its edge. During this long stillstand of the ice margin a second great line of glacial deposits of sand, gravel, clay, and boulders accumulated and Cape Cod came into being. On later pages we shall learn what these glacial deposits are made of and the various landscape features they now form.

LOBES OF ICE

Notice on the map (Figure 3) that the direction of ice movement was not everywhere the same. Along some lines the ice moved faster than on either side, so that the ice spread forward into an *ice lobe* having a curved front. Three ice lobes are of

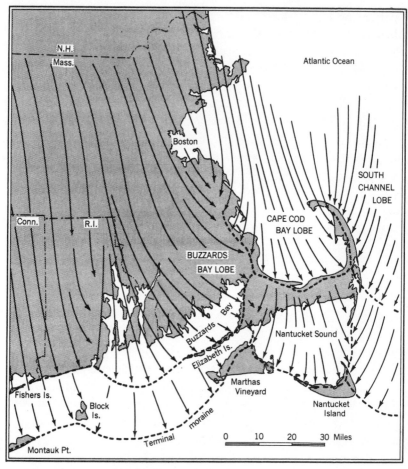

Atlantic Ocean

N.H.
Mass.

Boston

Conn.   R.I.

SOUTH
CHANNEL
LOBE

CAPE COD
BAY LOBE

BUZZARDS
BAY LOBE

Buzzards Bay

Elizabeth Is.

Nantucket Sound

Marthas
Vineyard

Fishers Is.

Block
Is.

Nantucket
Island

Terminal   moraine

0   10   20   30 Miles

Montauk Pt.

3. This map of southeastern New England shows by arrows the directions of flow of ice of the Wisconsin Stage as well as the two positions of ice stand-still (dashed lines). (Based on a map in Woodworth and Wigglesworth's *Geography and Geology of the Region Including Cape Cod*..., 1934.)

particular interest: the *Buzzards Bay Ice Lobe,* which spread forward into the area of Buzzards Bay; the *Cape Cod Bay Ice Lobe,* which occupied the lower ground of Cape Cod Bay; and the *South Channel Ice Lobe,* which spread southward over the ancient coastal plain to the east of the Cape.

Between these ice lobes the ice margin bent sharply into V-shaped notches pointed north. As would be expected, the deposits formed along the ice margin take the same outlines as the ice lobes, bowed southward into great arcs joined together at sharp V's pointed north. Now it becomes apparent that the lobes of the ice sheet had much to do with determining the outline of Cape Cod and of other closely related features such as Buzzards Bay, Marthas Vineyard, and Nantucket Island.

THE ICE SHEETS WASTE AWAY

Rather suddenly, about twelve thousand years ago, a rapid warming of the world climate set in and the ice sheets of North America and Europe began to waste away. New ice was no longer accumulating in the northern ice centers, so that the ice sheets ceased to spread southward and instead became stagnant or nearly motionless along their southern margins. Over New England the ice sheet rapidly lost thickness by melting and evaporation until it separated into individual ice masses and blocks.

Finally the last vestiges of ice were gone and the great work of the ice sheets in shaping Cape Cod had come to an end. Now the ice of the great continental ice sheets had been returned to the oceans in liquid form, causing the sea level to rise until a considerable part of the material deposited by the ice sheets was submerged and the shoreline had come to rest against the glacial deposits. The Atlantic Ocean thus entered Cape Cod Bay, Nantucket Sound, and Long Island Sound. The rising waters isolated Marthas Vineyard and Nantucket Island, which had been built of somewhat higher masses of glacial deposits (Figure 4). As we shall soon see, the final rise of sea level brought into being the period of work of waves and currents, which changed the shore-line of Cape Cod and gave the peninsula its final form.

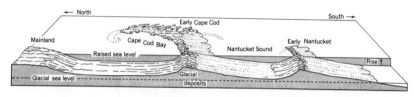

4. The front part of this block diagram shows a north-south belt running through Cape Cod and Nantucket Island. Glacial sea level is low, exposing the entire area. The rear part of the diagram shows conditions about thirty-five hundred years ago, when sea level had risen almost to its present position, filling Cape Cod Bay and Nantucket Sound, and producing the early shore-line of the modern Cape.

HOW THE ICE SHEETS CHANGED THE FACE OF
NEW ENGLAND

One can think of an ice sheet as acting much as a giant conveyor belt, bringing rock fragments southward to the ice margin and there depositing them in an ever-increasing pile (Figure 5). This happens because glacial ice moves only in one direction—from its source to its margin—so that material carried to the margin

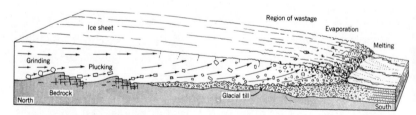

5. An ice sheet erodes by grinding and plucking of bedrock (left). In the region of wastage (right) the ice disappears through evaporation and melting, leaving its load of rock debris in the form of glacial till.

cannot be returned. The rock fragments contained in an ice sheet are obtained from the soil and bedrock of the region over which the ice passes. Ice exerts a grinding and dragging action on the land, like a great rasp. It also lifts out large joint blocks of bedrock, a process called *plucking*. Particles of clay, silt, sand, gravel, and many large boulders are in this way broken loose and mixed in with the lower layers of the moving ice to be carried far from their sources.

Much of New England was heavily scoured by the ice, so that not only was the soil and decomposed rock removed, but considerable solid bedrock was worn from exposed hills and mountain sides and summits. The ice carried this rock material southward toward Cape Cod. Of course, not all of the material reached the Cape, for much was deposited in New England valleys and lowlands. The Buzzards Bay Ice Lobe brought rock material southward across southeastern Massachusetts and across Buzzards Bay, to the region of the Elizabeth Islands and Woods Hole. The Cape Cod Ice Lobe not only brought rock material from the mainland, but also dragged along material from the floor of what is now Cape Cod Bay. The South Channel Ice Lobe seems to have brought its rock material from Maine and points north.

DEPOSITS LEFT BY THE ICE

Let us now study the forms of deposits of the rock matter brought to the ice margin. Any deposit of rock fragments carried by ice and later exposed by the melting and evaporation of the ice is called *glacial till*, or simply *till* (Figure 5). Two kinds can be recognized. First is the very dense mixture of clay, sand, and pebbles, with many boulders, which is dragged along at the base of the ice. This deposit is known as *basal till* and is usually rich in clay and is densely compacted (Figure 6). A second form of till is that which remains after the ice has completely melted and all of the suspended solid particles have settled out in a layer over the ground. This second form of till is called *residual till*, because it is a kind of solid residue. Residual till is usually softer and more

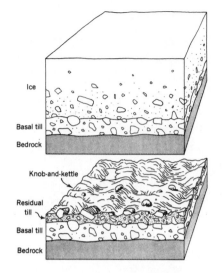

Ice

Basal till

Bedrock

Knob-and-kettle

Residual till

Basal till

Bedrock

6. In the upper block, debris-ladened ice lies above basal till. In the lower block, representing conditions after disappearance of the ice, a residual till layer lies upon the basal till. The knob-and-kettle landscape shown here is typical of most terminal moraines.

7. Enos Rock, Eastham, Massachusetts. This great glacial erratic measures about forty feet long and twenty-five feet wide. It rises over fifteen feet in height above ground level. The rock is a fine-grained greenish metamorphic type, possibly originally of volcanic origin, and has numerous fine veins of light-colored minerals. Enos Rock lies only a few yards south of the road leading from the Cape Cod National Seashore Visitor Center to Nauset Beach.   ARTHUR N. STRAHLER

8. Large erratic boulders, such as this one exposed at low tide, and many smaller ones as well, can be seen at Nauset Beach, where storm waves have undermined scarps of bouldery glacial till. ARTHUR N. STRAHLER

sandy than basal till, but it too has many large stones, including great boulders.

Large and conspicuous boulders in glacial till are sometimes called *glacial erratics* because they have been carried many miles distant from the bedrock in which they originated (Figure 7). For example, you will find on Cape Cod some erratic boulders composed of a pink granite, and these have come from the coast of Maine, some one hundred and fifty miles distant. A common sight on beaches of Cape Cod, Nantucket, and Marthas Vineyard is an apron of glacial boulders, derived from till in the scarps above the beach (Figure 8). Many of the pebbles, cobblestones, and boulders seen in the glacial till of Cape Cod show scratches, known as *glacial striations,* made by the scraping of one rock fragment against another, or against solid bedrock, as the ice moved (Figure 9).

9. This erratic boulder, found on the beach at Nauset Coast Guard Station, shows numerous glacial striations on its surface. (Sketched from a photograph in "Fossiliferous Tills and Intertill Beds of Cape Cod, Massachusetts" by Robert W. Sayles and Arthur S. Knox, 1943.)

Glacial till is found today spread over most of the region covered by the ice sheets of the Pleistocene Epoch, but is particularly thick close to the former ice sheet margins because of the conveyor-belt effect. As already stated, Cape Cod lies along one of the lines at which the ice margin stood for a long time. The result was that glacial till was built up into a broad belt of hills, known as a *moraine,* forming the backbone (geologically speaking) of Cape Cod, as well as of Marthas Vineyard and Nantucket (Figure 3).

THE MORAINE OF CAPE COD

On Cape Cod the glacial moraine followed the curvature of the fronts of the ice lobes and is not difficult to identify because it makes the highest ground on the Cape (much of it is above one hundred feet in elevation) and contains the highest hills, some of them rising over two hundred feet in elevation.

Let us follow the moraine across Cape Cod, starting at the southwest and ending on the east. The moraine enters Cape Cod at Woods Hole, which is on a peninsula pointed southwest toward the Elizabeth Islands (also made up of the moraine). From Woods Hole the moraine runs north-northeast as a hill belt one to two miles broad. The moraine passes east of West Falmouth and North Falmouth and you may drive right along it for several miles in this area on the newer highway section of Route 28.

There are many small hills and deep hollows in the moraine, so that the geologist sometimes refers to such a moraine landscape as *knob-and-kettle* (Figures 10 and 11). The "kettles" represent hollows which formed by the melting of large blocks of ice covered and surrounded by till. The moraine which we are describing as extending from Woods Hole, north-northeast to the Cape Cod Canal, has been named the *Buzzards Bay Moraine,* because it was

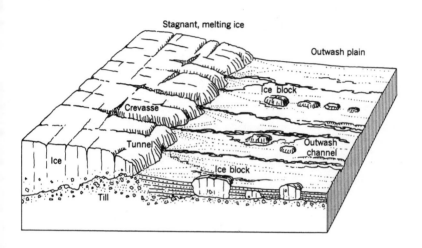

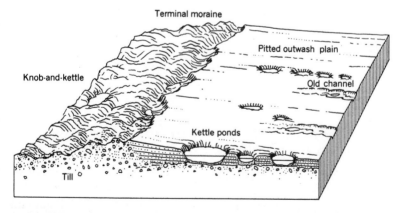

10. Conditions close to the margin of an almost stagnant ice sheet are shown diagrammatically in the upper block diagram. (The area shown might be two or three miles across.) The lower block diagram shows the same area after the ice is entirely gone. Terminal moraine lies on the left; pitted outwash plain on the right.

11. Knob-and-kettle landscape of the Buzzards Bay Moraine near Woods Hole, Massachusetts.   DOUGLAS JOHNSON

formed by the Buzzards Bay Ice Lobe. Some geologists have referred to this same deposit as the *Falmouth Moraine* from the township through which it passes (Figure 12).

In the vicinity of the Cape Cod Canal, where the Cape joins the mainland, the moraine makes a great bend to the east. This is the area near the town of Sandwich. Actually, the Mid-Cape Highway runs right along the moraine from the Cape Cod Canal eastward for at least fifteen miles, so that you have an excellent opportunity to see the moraine for much of its length. It's easy to see why the moraine was chosen as the place for the new highway. The sandy, hilly ground was never very attractive as a place to farm or build towns so it became a "desert" belt between the more desirable lower coastal fringes on either side.

The stretch of moraine which we are now following eastward is named the *Sandwich Moraine,* after the town of Sandwich, and represents the marginal position of the Cape Cod Ice Lobe. The Sandwich Moraine passes eastward through Barnstable, Yarmouth, and the Brewsters. In most of this stretch the moraine extends north as far as the shore of Cape Cod Bay. In the vicinity of Orleans the moraine extends across the entire Cape and reaches the Atlantic shore, where it can be seen in the steep bluffs back of Nauset Beach. How much farther the moraine once extended out into what is now the open Atlantic Ocean is not known, for the great waves of countless easterly storms have cut back the land since the ice sheet disappeared. It seems very likely that the moraine continued east for many miles along the margin of the Channel Ice Lobe.

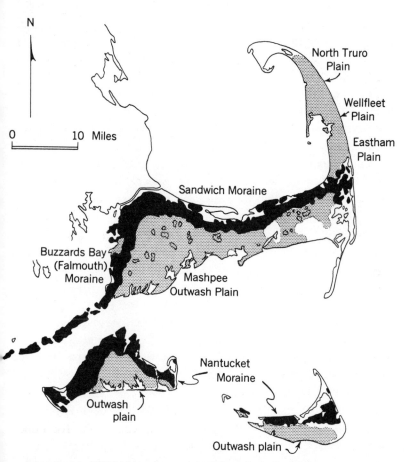

12. Moraines (solid black) and outwash plains (shaded) of Cape Cod, Marthas Vineyard, and Nantucket Island. (Based on geologic maps by Woodworth and Wigglesworth, 1934.)

THE OUTWASH PLAINS OF CAPE COD

East of the Buzzards Bay Moraine and extending all along the south side of the Sandwich Moraine is a broad, low plain of sand and gravel sloping gradually down to the south shoreline of the Cape on Nantucket Sound. This plain, called the Mashpee pitted outwash plain, has an elevation of eighty to one hundred feet where it lies next to the moraine, but falls gradually to about twenty feet elevation near the south shore (Figure 12). Many lakes are found scattered over the plain—Mashpee Pond, Santuit Pond, Peters Pond, and Wequaquet Lake, to mention only a few by name.

How did this plain of sand and gravel come into being? How is it related to the moraine away from which it slopes? To answer these questions we must imagine what was happening during the many hundreds, perhaps thousands of years during which the ice margin lay along the line of the Falmouth and Sandwich moraines. Despite the fact the world climate was considerably cooler than to-day and that Cape Cod then had a climate resembling that found in Baffin Island or Iceland today, during the summer seasons temperatures were well above the freezing point for many weeks of the year, causing the melting of enormous quantities of glacial ice. After all, the ice sheet could not have held its margin steady along the line of the moraine if melting and evaporation had not been fast enough to take away just as much ice as was gradually creeping southward from the thick ice centers over Canada.

So we can imagine that during the summers many vigorous streams and small rivers of meltwater flowed southward from the ice sheet across the ground lying to the south, and eventually reached the shoreline of the ocean. Some of these meltwater streams flowed over the ice surface (just as they do today on the margins of the Greenland Icecap); others came out from canyon-like ice gorges cut deep in the ice; still others emerged from tunnels roofed over by ice (Figure 10). Wherever and however the streams emerged, they had one activity in common: they carried much rock material, some in the form of the finest clay and silt, some as sand, gravel, and cobblestones moving close to the beds of the streams.

The fine clay and silt was held suspended in the turbulent water, which had a milky appearance. This fine material was mostly finely ground rock, known as *rock flour;* it traveled far and came to rest as clay and silt layers on the floor of the ocean, far beyond the limits of Cape Cod. On the other hand, the sand, gravel, and cobblestones moved distances of only a few hundred yards to several miles before coming permanently to rest. Summer after summer the meltwater streams built up the layers of sand and gravel to the south of the moraine. The layers sloped south very gently because the streams required a downhill slope on which to flow and transport the particles. Thus there gradually was built a sloping plain of a kind known to geologists as an *outwash plain.* This is the explanation of the broad plain stretching across the south side of Cape Cod. The very same process of outwash-plain building can be seen in action today at the edge of existing icecaps in Arctic lands.

Toward the close of the glacial stage, after the moraine and outwash plain had been built up to their present heights, some seasons of very rapid ice melting occurred, because the climate was now rapidly warming. There resulted some exceptionally great floods of meltwater from the remaining ice and these flood waters scoured several deep trench-like valleys across the outwash plain. Such valleys are called *outwash channels* (Figure 10). Today they are occupied by chains of small lakes and cranberry bogs. One good example of an outwash channel is the Bass River between Yarmouth and Dennis. Another smaller channel, about two miles east of Bass River, begins near Walkers Pond and runs south to Swan Pond (near Dennisport) where it continues as Swan Pond River and reaches Nantucket Sound.

LAKES AND PONDS OF THE OUTWASH PLAIN

But what about the many lakes and large ponds which are scattered about over the outwash plain? It is quite out of the

13. A group of small kettle ponds just south of Queen Anne Road, Harwich, Massachusetts. Bucks Pond and Josephs Pond are the two most distant ones.

These ponds average about one thousand feet in width. The view is about
due west.   HAROLD L. R. COOPER, CAPE COD PHOTOS

question to think that the streams of meltwater just happened to miss the lake basins, building up the plain around those places, because meltwater streams are of a broad, shallow type that easily spreads from side to side, filling in all hollows that may be present in the plain. Then again, one might guess that the lake and pond basins were formed long after the ice sheet was gone, in other words, that somehow the sand was excavated at certain places to make basins for lakes. However, many of the ponds are surrounded on all sides by rather steep walls and there is no evidence of any process that would take out the sand so neatly (Figure 13).

To unravel the mystery of the lakes and ponds, use a clue given some pages back in this book. Remember that the ice sheet once reached farther south than Cape Cod, coming to rest along a line on which Marthas Vineyard and Nantucket are now located (Figure 3). These islands consist of moraine and outwash plain, very much like Cape Cod, but they were formed first, for the ice sheet spread to its farthest south limit first. Then in a period of less cool climate the ice margin wasted back to the line of the moraine on Cape Cod. What this all means is that there was for some time an ice sheet covering the south side of Cape Cod as well as Nantucket Sound. When the ice in that area was melted, there remained many great blocks of glacial ice, scattered over the area of the southern side of Cape Cod. These ice blocks, which were from a small fraction of a mile across to as much as a mile or more across, remained in place while the meltwater streams of the Buzzards Bay and Sandwich ice lobes were building the Cape Cod outwash plain.

Now, the meltwater streams would have flowed around the ice blocks, building up the sand higher and higher around the ice blocks. Eventually the smaller blocks were completely buried in sand. Later, after the meltwater streams had ceased to flow, the ice blocks melted completely away leaving cavities in the sand (Figure 10). Such cavities, or pits, would have very steep sides and no outlets. The sand and gravel would later slide and roll down the sides of the cavities, making the walls less steep, but there remained no flowing streams to bring sediment into the cavities. The geologist refers to the hollows and lakes thus pro-

14. Round Pond, a small but deep kettle pond near U. S. Highway 6, north of Wellfleet. See Figure 43 for a map of this area.   ARTHUR N. STRAHLER

duced as *ice-block lakes,* or *kettles.* Almost every lake on Cape Cod (except some near the shore which are tidal lagoons or bays) is an ice-block lake. A particularly fine example of a very deep, though small, kettle which can be easily examined from the main highway is Round Pond, on Route 6, two and a half miles north of Wellfleet (Figure 14).

Some of the ice-block depressions do not contain fresh-water ponds or lakes, but instead are bays connected with the sea. A fine example is Town Cove, at Orleans. Another is Salt Pond, easily seen from U. S. Highway 6 in Eastham. Still another such bay is Drummer Cove at South Wellfleet. In general, we can use the local name "salt pond" for any ice-block depressions connected to the sea by tidal channels, to distinguish them from the "fresh-water ponds" whose surfaces are at least several feet above sea level.

PLAINS OF EASTHAM, WELLFLEET, AND TRURO

So far, little attention has been paid to the outer part of Cape Cod—the part pointing north and making the forearm of the peninsula. This is the portion between Orleans and North Truro. Most of this part of the Cape consists of sand and gravel plains which prove to be outwash plains. In some places (for example, around North Eastham) the plain is very smooth. In other places (for example, from South Wellfleet to Truro) the plain is very rough, with many kettles and ice-block lakes.

Whatever the surface—rough or smooth—this section of Cape Cod has a very interesting feature that quickly catches the eye of the geologist as he studies his maps of the Cape. The feature that we are referring to is the general slope from high ground on the east shore to lower ground on the west shore. As all visitors to the Cape quickly learn, the east shore of this part of Cape Cod is almost continuously bordered by a great sand cliff, or scarp, which is usually one hundred or more feet high and in places considerably more. The highest points on the eastern Cape are along the top of this sea scarp. Not only does the outwash plain slope westward toward Cape Cod Bay, but a number of outwash channels and stream valleys cross the Cape from east to west.

If the eastern part, or forearm, of Cape Cod is composed of glacial outwash, where is the moraine which should lie next to it, marking the position of the margin of the ice? We should expect a moraine along the east side of the outwash plain, but instead there is only the great scarp of sand. Perhaps at this point you have already guessed the explanation. The moraine must have been cut away by the action of storm waves of the open Atlantic Ocean. Evidence for such cutting-back is given in later pages.

Although the full geologic story of the eastern part of Cape Cod is not known, it is reasonable for us to think that the outwash sand and gravel found on the forearm of the Cape came from stagnant, melting ice of the Channel Ice Lobe which lay east of the Cape (rather than from the Cape Cod Ice Lobe) because the surface of the outwash plain slopes from east to west, requiring that the source of the sand and gravel be located on the Atlantic Ocean side of the Cape. Also, the many outwash channels that cut across the Cape have floors that slope westward, showing that the meltwater came from a body of ice lying to the east.

Those of you who have walked along the base of the steep

scarp at Highland Light near North Truro may have noticed that some of the layers exposed in the cliff contain boulders and that in places there is much clay. In other words, there is glacial till on the eastern arm of Cape Cod and it lies buried under the outwash plain sands and gravels. Glacial till is also seen at other points in the scarp farther south, for example at a point a half mile south of the Pamet River Coast Guard Station and at the Nauset Beach Lighthouse. To the geologist the finding of glacial till at these various points along the scarp running down the eastern coast of the Cape means that a moraine lies buried beneath the outwash plain. How does this moraine fit into the pattern of the moraine as it has already been outlined? Evidently the buried moraine of the forearm of Cape Cod was formed between the Cape Cod Bay Ice Lobe and the South Channel Ice Lobe along the line where the two bodies of ice met. Such a deposit is known as *interlobate moraine,* that is, a "moraine-between-lobes" (see Figure 3).

What the Waves Have Done

SEA LEVEL RISES

As the great ice sheets wasted away during the rapid warming of climate, which set in about twelve thousand years ago, the level of the sea rose rapidly, bringing the shoreline higher and higher upon the moraine and outwash plains of Cape Cod. By about thirty-five hundred years ago the sea had reached nearly to its present level along the southern New England coast (Figure 4 and Figure 15). We can imagine that a map of the Cape then looked like a piece of Swiss cheese, its many bays forming a ragged, scalloped shoreline. Of course, the ragged shoreline shown in Figure 15 is largely guesswork and is meant only to give a general idea of the form of the shoreline. The bays were the ice-block hollows or kettles explained on earlier pages. The soft sand, gravel, and clay of our piece of Swiss cheese was a tempting meal placed before the hungry storm waves of the Atlantic Ocean; the feasting began at once.

INCOMING WAVES

Ocean waves are made by wind, which drags against the water surface over which it blows. Energy of the wind is thus transferred to energy of waves. A part of this energy travels through the water in the direction the waves are moving. Now, as everyone knows who has been out in a small boat on the sea, or on a large lake, the water itself does not travel along with the waves. There is only a small forward and backward motion of the water as each wave passes; only the shape of the wave travels through the water. Perhaps, then, ocean waves in deep water should be thought of as making a broad, shallow "river" of flowing energy, but not of flowing water. When a nor'easter (a storm in which winds come from the northeast) is blowing over the New England coast, the "river" of wave energy flows toward Cape Cod.

What happens to this "energy-river" as the waves approach the shallow water of the coast? First, the waves begin to feel the sea floor and drag against it. This is a form of friction that takes energy from the waves and slows them down. In shallow water, as a wave crest passes, water at the sea bottom flows landward, dragging along sand; as the following wave trough passes the bottom current is reversed and flows seaward, dragging the sand seaward. This continual back-and-forth dragging action by waves in shallow water causes the sand to develop *ripple marks,* the tiny wavelets of sand which can be seen through clear water (Figure 16). The back-and-forth drag can also move the sand along for great distances, for, if the seaward drag under the wave troughs is stronger than the landward drag, the sand grains will gradually move out to deeper water offshore. It is by this action that the waves have been able to dispose of much of the sand and gravel cut from the cliffs of Cape Cod.

N

10 Miles

15. The solid line shows a hypothetical shoreline of eastern Cape Cod, as it might have existed about thirty-five hundred years ago. The dashed line shows the present shoreline. (Based in part on a figure in Davis' "The Outline of Cape Cod," 1896.)

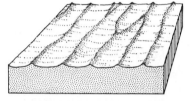

16. Ripple marks in fine sand on the floor of the shallow offshore zone. Here the effect of passing waves is felt as a back-and-forth drag. These ripples measure three to five inches from crest to crest. (Sketched from a photograph by the author.)

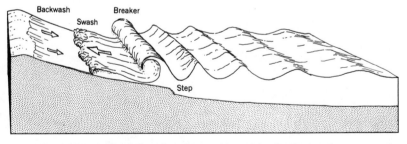

17. This highly stylized drawing shows changes in the form of a wave as it approaches the shore. After collapse of the breaker the water rides up the beach as swash, then reverses flow to become the backwash.

As the waves are followed into even shallower water it is seen that they are becoming higher and more closely spaced (Figure 17). This change also means that front and back slopes of the waves are becoming steeper. Then, quite suddenly, the steep-sided wave can no longer hold its shape. The top part leaps forward and falls into a line of foaming, swirling water—the *breaker* we all know so well. But after the breaker has collapsed it becomes a mass of water moving rapidly forward toward the beach or cliff. Now we see that the same wave which in deep water moved so quietly under our boat, rocking us very gently, has become a great battering ram hurling tons of water toward the shore. This, then, is how the energy of the waves has finally changed its method of travel as it comes to the end of its long journey across the ocean.

The foaming, swirling surge of water that the breaker creates is known as the *swash* (Figure 17). On the sand beaches of Cape Cod, which have a rather steep slope as sand beaches go, the swash is forced to run uphill, against the force of gravity, so that the water quickly slows down and finally comes to a halt. Much of the water sinks into the porous sand, but that which does not sink in begins to flow back down the slope of the beach to become the *backwash*. You don't need to be told that the swash and backwash sweep sand, gravel, and cobbles first up the beach slope, then back down, for you have seen this happen countless times (Figure 18).

PARTS OF A BEACH

If you will be spending a good part of your vacation time on the fine beaches of Cape Cod, it might be a good idea to learn something about the parts of a beach and how they originate. These parts are largest and best developed on the beaches of the eastern shore of the Cape, where the action of waves is strongest, but the principles apply to all marine sand beaches. The steeply sloping sand surface over which the swash and backwash continually sweep is called the *foreshore* (Figure 19). For beaches of medium-grade sand, the foreshore may have a slope of about 1 in 10, meaning that it drops one foot for each ten feet of horizontal distance. For very fine sand the slope would be much lower; for cobblestones, much steeper. At the base of the foreshore, where the innermost breakers form, there is often a deposit of coarse gravel and cobblestones, taking either the form of a bench, known as a *step* (shown in Figure 17), or of a low ridge called a *submarine bar* (Figure 19). Beyond the foreshore lies a zone called the *offshore,* which has a gentle slope of finer sand and is exposed only when the tide falls to unusually low water.

At the upper, landward edge of the foreshore lies the *summer berm,* which is a terrace of sand, sometimes nearly flat, in other instances having a crest and a slight landward slope. The summer berm is built of sand which is brought up with the swash and left stranded at the high-water mark of the swash. The summer berm gradually widens during the summer when waves are small, but may be quickly cut back or even entirely removed by the strong swash and backwash of a tropical storm. Landward of the summer berm there lies a still higher terrace of sand, the *winter berm,* built by the larger waves accompanying winter storms. On some broad sand beaches there are several of these higher berms, each stepping up slightly higher than the one next to it. The winter berm is sometimes completely cut away by severe storms, only to be rebuilt again. Few plants will grow on the winter berm, and it may have an accumulation of large driftwood logs at its inner margin. Landward of the berms lies the belt of sand dunes, which is not part of the beach, but represents a zone of higher ground built by wind action.

As many of you know, there are times when the beach shows a series of shallow bays and points giving a scalloped appearance to the summer berm and foreshore slope. These irregularities are called *beach cusps* (Figure 20). Very little is known as to just how and why beach cusps form and disappear, but it seems to have something to do with the height and direction of approach of the waves and the range of rise and fall of tide. Cusps may form in a period of a few days, then disappear and leave a regular beach surface for another period of several days.

18. In this air view of The Provincelands dunes, we see Atlantic storm waves breaking obliquely against the shoreline. The direction in which sand is

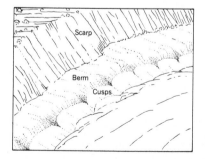

20. Beach cusps.

being moved is from upper left to lower right (eastward), toward Race Point. This is a winter scene and the dunes are snow-covered.

HAROLD L. R. COOPER, CAPE COD PHOTOS

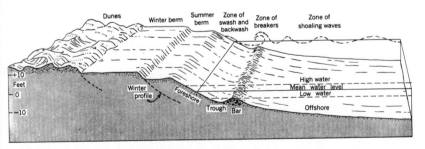

19. Typical parts of a sand beach are shown here in diagrammatic form to represent summer conditions.

STORM WAVE EROSION

Getting back to the story of Cape Cod, the period of time immediately following the rise of sea level was one of great attack by storm waves and the rapid removal of the projecting points and peninsulas of glacial material. The geologist uses the term *erosion* to mean the wearing away and removal of any kind of earth material by the action of one of Nature's four agents of erosion: streams, waves, glacial ice, and wind. At the moment we are particularly interested in *wave erosion,* or *marine erosion,* and how it shaped the coastline of Cape Cod.

The swash of breaking storm waves acts like a great saw blade held flat on its side so as to cut nearly horizontally into the land. The storm swash is so powerful that it easily rides up the sloping beach and strikes a great blow at the steeper ground which lies back of the beach. The returning backwash sweeps the sand seaward and it is gradually moved out into deeper water, where it comes to rest. The swash thus tries to cut a notch in the land, but because the glacial deposits of Cape Cod lack the strength to stand in a vertical wall, the slope above the notch keeps moving back by the continual rolling and sliding down of individual grains or by the slipping down of block-like masses (Figure 21). As the material reaches the beach at the base of the slope it is taken away by the storm swash and backwash.

MARINE SCARPS OF CAPE COD

Those parts of the Cape Cod shoreline which were most exposed to storm waves were cut back into steep *marine scarps* or *sea scarps.* The word "scarp" means an abrupt, steep slope that extends for a long distance. Sometimes the terms *marine cliffs,* or *sea cliffs,* are applied to the marine scarps of Cape Cod, but the word "cliff" implies a nearly vertical wall, usually of hard rock. We find true marine cliffs along the Maine coast at Mount Desert Island, for example, where a very strong, hard pink granite forms the coast (Figure 21). Such rock can easily stand as a

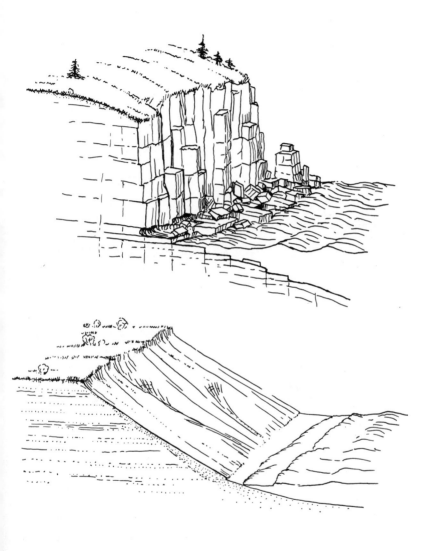

21. The nearly vertical marine cliff shown above is typical of the granite coast of Maine, while the gentler marine scarp of sand and gravel shown below is seen on Cape Cod. (From field sketches by the author.)

vertical wall many tens or even hundreds of feet high, but the glacial materials cannot. Generally you will find that the marine scarps of Cape Cod at such places as the Highland Light at North Truro or the Nauset Beach Light form a slope which has an angle of about thirty-four degrees from the horizontal because the

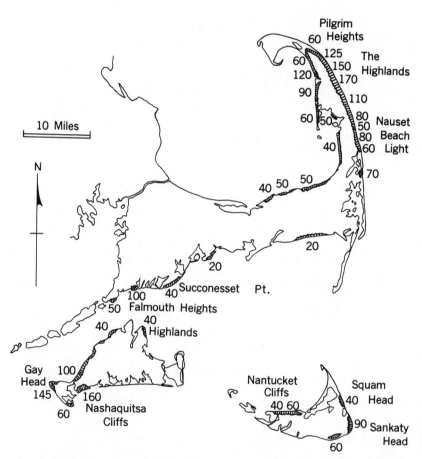

22. The principal marine scarps of Cape Cod, Marthas Vineyard, and Nantucket Island are indicated on this map by a hachured symbol adjacent to the shoreline. Approximate heights of the scarp at various places are given in feet. (Data from maps of the U. S. Geological Survey.)

sand and gravel constantly roll and slide and cannot stand at a
steeper angle (Figure 21). There are exceptions, of course, where
clay or mixtures of clay and sand of glacial till are exposed in the
scarps. Such fine material holds moisture and is said to have
cohesion, or a property of sticking together. Cohesion allows the
material to stand in a much steeper wall so that in places there
are small cliffs in clay to be found along the Cape Cod coastline.

Today the shoreline which extends about north–south along the
eastern side of Cape Cod is a smooth, broadly curving line which
gradually turns westward toward its northern end (Figure 22).
Along this shoreline is an almost continuous marine scarp, from
fifty to one hundred and fifty feet high along much of its length.
How did the original shoreline of the Cape, which we imagine to
have been at first ragged and irregular with many points and
bays, come to be so smoothed and simplified? The process needs
to be explained because it has happened along many coastlines of
the world. The basic law of science which acts to change a shoreline may be stated as follows: waves direct their strongest attack
upon capes and headlands which project into the sea, whereas
their attack is at the same time greatly weakened upon the shores
of bays. The result is that the projecting capes are cut back
rapidly while the bays are little affected. Finally a smooth, simple
shoreline will result.

WAVE REFRACTION

As explained before, waves coming into shallow water are slowed
down by friction with the sea floor. When waves approach a
coastline which consists of both bays and headlands, the waves
usually encounter shallow water first directly in front of the headlands and therefore are slowed down first at those places. Opposite
the bays, where water is deeper, the waves are not slowed down
and move right along with the original speed. The result is that
the line of the wave's crest becomes bent (Figure 23). Scientists
call such bending *wave refraction.* To help understand why bending must occur, think of a straight line of people with arms locked

together marching at the same speed across a flat plain. Suppose that the line crosses a patch of soft sand or mud which slows down the marchers who have to cross it. Of course the line of people will now be bent around the patch of soft ground. The shallow water which lies off a headland or cape acts in just the same manner and the waves are bent around it. Now there is another law of science that when the waves are bent into a form which is concave in the direction the waves are moving, the energy within the waves is increased, while at the same time energy is decreased in waves that are bent convexly outward. Consequently wave bending in front of a headland increases the height of the waves there and the breakers are higher and more powerful

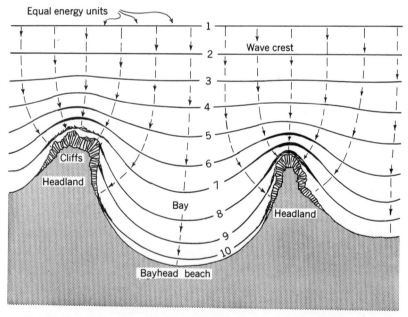

23. In this sketch map, looking down upon a section of rugged coastline, the refraction pattern of approaching waves is seen in the changes of crest lines of successive waves, numbered 1 through 10. Equal units of wave energy along crest Number 1 are gradually concentrated into narrower zones in front of the headlands, but are spread over broader zones opposite the bays.

there than elsewhere. Within the bays, on the other hand, the waves are made lower and by the time they reach the bay shore are much weakened.

CAPE COD HAS LOST GROUND

The result of wave bending and the concentrating of the force of the breakers upon the headlands and points is that those features are quickly cut back, whereas the shorelines of the bays are little affected by erosion. It is then only a matter of time before wave erosion entirely removes the projecting headlands and makes a smooth, simple shoreline which is straight or very broadly curved. In the past three thousand to four thousand years during which waves have acted upon Cape Cod the entire eastern shore of the forearm of the Cape has been heavily attacked, cut back, and shaped into the broadly sweeping curve found today. How far to the east did the headlands and promontories originally extend? We have no way to determine exactly how far; we can only guess that some points may have stood at least one to two miles farther east than the present shore.

What is the evidence that the eastern shore of Cape Cod has been cut back as much as two miles? If the land is not there now, how can one prove that it was ever there? Two quite different kinds of evidence can be brought forward. First is the measured rate of retreat of the marine scarp in historic time; second is the interpretation of certain valley features of this part of the Cape.

During the nineteenth century the United States Coast and Geodetic Survey undertook a study of the rate of retreat of the eastern shore of Cape Cod between the Highland Light and the Nauset Light (Figure 24). It was found that in the forty-year period between 1848 and 1888 the average distance of westward shift of the shoreline was 128 feet, which is at a rate of about three feet per year. It was estimated that in forty years the face of the scarp lost altogether about thirty million cubic yards of material for its entire length of about fourteen miles. This rate comes out to an average loss of about 750,000 cubic yards each year, or about 54,000 cubic yards for each mile of shore (Figure 25).

24. The Highlands of Capc Cod. This view northward shows the marine scarp, which is about one hundred and thirty feet high at this point. The Cape Cod Light is situated to the upper left, just outside the limits of this view.   ARTHUR N. STRAHLER

It is quite risky to use the figure of three feet of retreat per year to apply for long spans of time past or future, but if we do so, it turns out that two miles of coastal retreat would take thirty-five hundred years. Most geologists consider that the sea had reached to within ten or fifteen feet of its present level by about thirty-five hundred years ago. Thus our guess of a shoreline formerly as much as two miles farther east of the present one is a reasonable one in the light of present observations (Figure 15).

Other studies have shown rates of retreat of as high as five to eight feet per year for parts of this same shoreline. Using the figure of three feet per year to estimate the future changes, it can be predicted that the outer Cape will be entirely cut through at its narrowest point, which is near South Wellfleet, in some two thousand years. Remember that this is no more than a wild guess, for the rates observed today may not represent a long-term average and may change greatly as time passes.

HANGING VALLEYS

The second type of evidence of more land to the east is from valleys that cross Cape Cod from east to west at a number of places between North Truro and Wellfleet. Now, a normal stream valley with its tributaries will, as we follow it upstream, steepen to the place of encounter with the drainage divide, or watershed, which separates that valley from another sloping away in the opposite direction. If we follow the cross-valleys of eastern Cape Cod eastward, which is the direction of rising level of the valley floors, we find that the valleys end abruptly at the great marine scarp, making deep notches in that scarp. Such a valley ending abruptly in a scarp or cliff is known as a *hanging valley,* and is evidence that the valley formerly extended much farther than at present.

A fine example of a hanging valley is found at the eastern end of the Little Pamet River, which lies one mile north of Truro (Figure 26). If you take the Long Nook Road east from the Mid-Cape Highway, you will be following the rising floor of the Little Pamet River valley, ascending at a rate of about forty feet in a distance of one mile. At the end of the road you will find yourself in a hanging valley overlooking the Atlantic Ocean. The hanging valley stands about fifty-five feet above the sea. The size of the valley where it is abruptly ended leads to the guess that it may have extended a mile or so farther east.

A still more interesting cross-valley is that of the Pamet River, a flat-floored valley containing salt marsh and a meandering tidal stream, with no real gradient at all (Figure 26). This valley is obviously an old outwash channel, eroded by floods from melting ice which once lay to the east. The valley floor is just as broad at the east end as the west, and seems to be abruptly cut off by the Atlantic shoreline. From this we guess that there was more land to the east. Today a barrier of beach sands and dunes lies across the eastern end of the valley. It would be a very small feat of

25. Seen from a small plane, the seventy-foot marine scarp at Nauset Beach Lighthouse shows slopes of loose dry sand, which slid down the steep face following undercutting by storm waves. In this view, which is toward

the west, we can see entirely across the Cape to Cape Cod Bay, three miles distant.

HAROLD L. R. COOPER, CAPE COD PHOTOS

engineering to remove this low barrier and form a tide-level connection right across the Cape, but a much more difficult problem would be to keep the passage from being sealed across by more sand.

From examples offered by the Pamet River and Little Pamet River valleys, geologists have coined the term *pamet* to mean an outwash channel carved in glacial drift and having irregularities resulting from melting of blocks of stagnant ice.

MARINE SCARPS OF CAPE COD BAY AND NANTUCKET SOUND

Although the great marine scarp on the eastern shore of Cape Cod is the most obvious feature of wave erosion on the Cape, there are also many miles of wave-cut scarps along the inner or Cape Cod Bay shoreline (see Figure 22). These scarps begin at Pilgrim Heights, in a point known as High Head, between North Truro and Provincetown. Today the scarps which run both east and south from High Head are protected by more recent deposits, formed by waves and wind, which are explained on later pages. From the south end of Pilgrim Beach there extends southward a marine scarp which is now being cut by waves. In places this scarp is fifty to one hundred feet high. It can be followed with interruptions to Wellfleet Harbor. South of Wellfleet Harbor the coastline is abruptly set back some three miles farther east. Here, opposite North Eastham, begins another scarp, but this one is lower in height. Where the Bay shoreline turns westward, near Rock Harbor, the wave-cut scarps are missing for, as our laws of wave erosion state, the curved shoreline of a bay receives only weakened waves and rarely shows scarps of erosion.

As we travel west along the Bay shoreline of Brewster, Dennis, and Yarmouth we find more stretches of low erosion scarps, carved into the northern fringe of the Sandwich Moraine. It is not surprising that the marine scarps which border Cape Cod Bay are lower and less rapidly eroded than the great scarp of the Atlantic shore. Storm winds blowing across Cape Cod Bay can form waves over a water expanse of only a few tens of miles; therefore the breakers cannot attain the great size and energy of those formed over the open Atlantic.

Marine erosion has also cut back the south shore of Cape Cod at many places, producing wave-cut scarps and greatly simplifying what must have been a very irregular shoreline produced by ice-block depressions and outwash channels. Erosion has been greatest in the stretch of coast from Falmouth to Cotuit. A marine scarp is very well developed at Falmouth Heights; another on Great Neck at Succonesset. As we travel eastward along the south shore the sheltering effect of Monomoy Point, a long peninsula of sand which runs south from Chatham, has greatly reduced the amount of marine erosion, but because the outwash plain is very low here, the coastline has been very nicely smoothed and simplified.

Marine scarps of Marthas Vineyard and Nantucket are also shown on the map, Figure 22. The cliffs of Gay Head, at the western extremity of Marthas Vineyard, are particularly striking both for their variegated pastel colors and for their geological significance. Much of the colorful material exposed in the Gay Head Marine Scarp is clay of Cretaceous age (about seventy-five million years old) and is therefore vastly older than any deposits exposed on Cape Cod. What shows at Gay Head today is merely the crest of a belt of coastal hills that existed before the coming of the ice and the depression of the land under its weight. As the ice passed over the hill summits, its enormous pressure contorted the plastic clay layers into wave-like folds.

BEACH DRIFTING

Imagine that you are standing at the top of the marine scarp at The Highlands of Cape Cod, looking down upon the beach below (Figure 24). On most occasions in summer you will see that the waves which move toward the beach are not coming directly toward the shore. That is to say, instead of the wave crests being exactly parallel with the shoreline, they are oblique to the shoreline. A particular wave will make a narrow V with the line of the shore. The point of this V is toward the south and the angle of the V may measure from five to fifteen degrees. As a result, the breaking of a wave does not occur at the same instant along the entire wave, but occurs first where the wave is close to shore, near the apex of the V; the breaking seems to travel along the wave. Actually, the point of breaking is decided by the depth of water and stays fixed while the wave crosses the line of breaking depth.

The oblique approach of waves results from the fact that the direction of travel of the waves from the open sea is determined by the direction of the wind which forms the waves or, in the case of a swell, by the direction of the distant source of the waves. In summer along the Atlantic coast of the United States waves and swells most commonly approach from the southeast. In many winter storms—those which are nor'easters—the wind blows from the northeast, bringing in the waves from that direction.

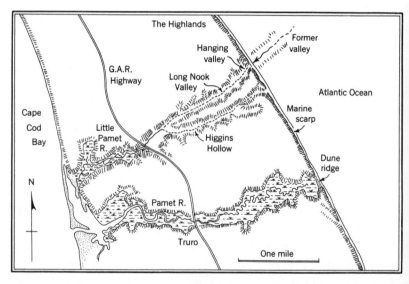

26. This sketch map of the Truro-Highlands area of Cape Cod shows cross-valleys of the Pamet and Little Pamet rivers. (Based on maps of the U. S. Geological Survey.)

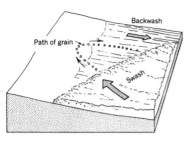

27. This block diagram of a small area of sand beach shows how a pebble or grain of sand is moved through an arched path with each swash and backwash.

When waves are approaching a shoreline obliquely, the swash from the breaking wave does not ride straight up the beach at right angles to the shoreline, but rather is thrust obliquely up the beach. Sand and pebbles are moved in the same direction. As the swash slows down the water seems to turn parallel with the shoreline for an instant, then reverses to flow obliquely back down the beach as the backwash (Figure 27). In other words, the water describes a curving path—like an arch—instead of a simple back-and-forth path on one line. Sand and pebbles also follow the curving path.

Obviously a grain of sand will in this way be moved along the beach as well as up and down it. Think now of millions of grains of sand and gravel, as well as countless pebbles and cobbles, moving in curving paths with each breaking wave. The total result is a great flow of rock particles in one direction along the beach, in some ways quite like the movement of sand and gravel in the bed of a swift river. This process of movement of sand along a beach is termed *beach drifting*.

THE LONGSHORE CURRENT

There is also a related kind of movement of rock particles along the shore, taking place in the shallow water of the zone of the steepening and breaking waves. The oblique approach of waves sets up a flow of water, known as a *longshore current,* flowing in the direction of the open end of the V made by the wave crests and the shoreline (Figure 28). A longshore current can reach a speed of three knots (about as fast as a medium walk) and in many ways acts like a river, dragging sand along the bottom parallel with the shore. The longshore current always moves sand in the same direction as does beach drifting (for a particular set of waves) so that the two processes work hand in hand to transport material along the shore. This combined process of transportation is called simply *shore drifting*. (Some geologists and engineers use the term *littoral drifting*.)

SAND BARS AND SANDSPITS

Now that we have seen how material can be moved in one or the other direction along a shoreline we can understand what becomes of much of the glacial sand, gravel, and cobbles cut away from the marine scarps by storm waves. This material simply moves along the shore until it can find a place to come to rest. Where the shoreline undergoes a sharp landward bend, as it would at the end of a cape, or where the mouth of a bay is reached, the

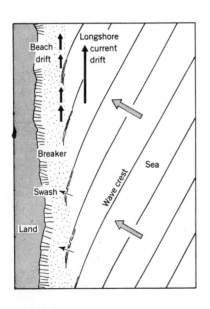

28. A sketch map to show how the oblique approach of waves causes sand to be transported simultaneously in the same direction by beach drifting and longshore-current drifting.

shore drifting of material, instead of following the sharp turn, continues on in a more or less straight line, right out into deeper water (Figure 29). The deeper the water, the weaker the shore drifting becomes, so that the grains of sand soon come to a place where they can move no farther. The result is the formation of a *sand bar* under the water. The sand bar grows in length and is also built up above water level by swash and backwash until it becomes a *sandspit,* which is simply a long, narrow ridge of sand projecting out into deeper water and forming a continuation of the part of the beach from which the material is coming. Almost without exception, a sandspit will have a curved form, bending toward the land at its outer tip. Geologists say that the spit is *recurved.*

Now let us look for some examples of rather simple sand bars and recurved spits which have been built on Cape Cod by shore drifting. Nauset Beach can illustrate the principles very nicely. From the marine scarp in the area of the Nauset Beach Light, the southward shore drifting of material has taken place when waves approach from the northeast (Figure 30). At Nauset Bay

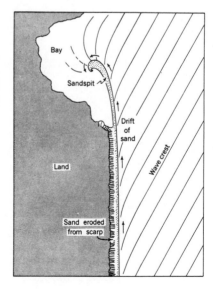

29. This map of a section of coast-line shows how a sandspit is constructed by the shore drift of sand continued out into the open water of a bay.

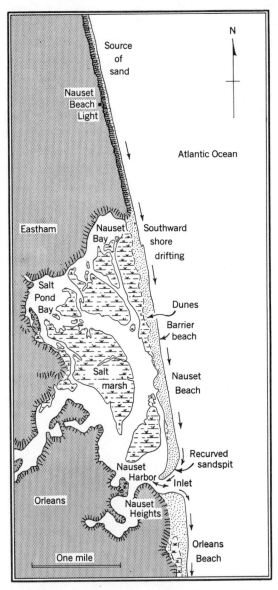

30. Sketch map of the Nauset coast of eastern Cape Cod showing the barrier beach built of sand which has drifted southward. (Based on maps of the U. S. Geological Survey.)

a long, narrow sandspit was built southward, continuing the line of the marine scarp on the north. This sandspit finally reached a length of over two miles, completely shutting off Nauset Bay from the open Atlantic and leaving only a narrow opening, or *inlet,* at the mouth of Nauset Harbor.

When a sandspit has extended itself almost completely across a bay, we refer to the whole deposit instead as a *baymouth bar* (also called a *barrier bar* or *barrier beach*). The spit itself is now only the low end portion of the bar which ends in open water. From Nauset Heights, looking north across the opening of Nauset Harbor, you can see the low sandspit, curved landward. It represents the end of the baymouth bar, which is receiving sand brought south by shore drifting. Tidal currents, which are referred to later, sweep this sand landward and seaward from the tip of the spit, so that it now is growing only very slowly, or not at all.

From Nauset Heights the southward drift of sand has formed a continuation of Nauset Beach as a barrier beach which blocks off Little Pleasant Bay and its islands from the open sea. Still farther south this barrier beach becomes a long narrow peninsula enclosing Pleasant Bay and lying east of Chatham, which it protects from the open sea. Nauset Beach ends in a long, low recurved sandspit which continues to be built southward.

MONOMOY ISLAND

A still larger body of sand built by shore drifting is Monomoy Island, jutting eight miles south from Chatham into Nantucket Sound (Figure 31). Monomoy Island is a rather complicated sandspit consisting of several curving ridges of sand joined together and now covered with dunes formed by wind. Each ridge represents a former beach. As more and more sand was drifted south one beach was added seaward of the former ones and the sandspit was pushed farther and farther south into Nantucket Sound.

The sand which is now being added to Monomoy Point is

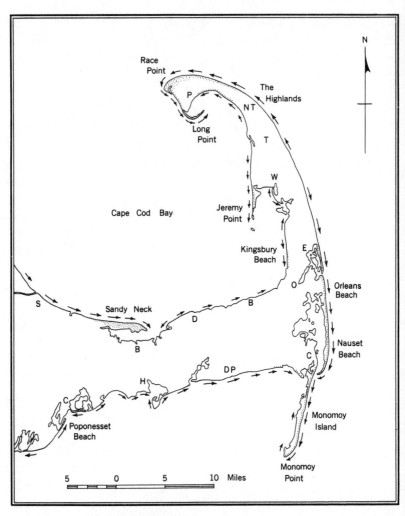

31. Arrows paralleling the shore show the prevailing directions of shore drifting of sand on this map of Cape Cod. The single letters are abbreviations of community names. (Based on a map by Woodworth, 1934, with added details from the author's interpretation of recent maps by the U. S. Geological Survey.)

probably brought all the way south from the high marine scarps in the Nauset-Wellfleet area. It moves south along Nauset Beach to the end of that spit near Chatham, then is carried across the mouth of Pleasant Bay by tidal currents to reach Monomoy Beach. The sand is moved south during northeast storms. As an example of how fast this happens, during the twelve years between 1856 and 1868 Monomoy Point was extended southward at a rate of one hundred and fifty-seven feet per year.

The accompanying map shows by arrows the directions of shore drifting elsewhere on Cape Cod (Figure 31).

TOMBOLOS OF WELLFLEET HARBOR

If you will follow the shoreline of Cape Cod Bay southward from Truro, you will find that the low marine scarp gives way to a succession of islands. These are named Bound Brook Island, Griffin Island, Great Island, and Great Beach Hill. All four of these islands are bold hill masses of glacial drift with well-developed marine scarps overlooking Cape Cod Bay. But these islands are actually connected in a chain. The connecting links are narrow barrier beaches of sand with bordering belts of dune and tidal marsh. The connecting beach between Griffin Island and Great Island is named The Gut. Although called "islands," the hills of drift are not truly islands today because they have been joined to one another and to the mainland by sand carried southward by beach drifting and ending in Jeremy Point, a recurved sandspit (Figure 31).

Land-tied islands are found in many places along the world's coasts. In Italy, where any beach may be called a *tombolo,* a number of good examples can be seen. Geologists writing in English have long used the term *tombolo* as a scientific word to mean a sand beach or bar connecting an island with the mainland or with other islands. The tombolos along Cape Cod Bay west of Wellfleet Harbor are fine examples of their kind. You can see them from high vantage points on public roads west of the town of Wellfleet.

GROWTH OF THE PROVINCELANDS

By far the most interesting and spectacular deposit made by the shore drifting of sand is known as *The Provincelands,* and forms the "wrist" and "fist" of the Cape Cod arm, enclosing Provincetown Harbor. As we have seen, the glacial deposits end in High Head at Pilgrim Heights, where there exists old marine scarps cut by storm waves soon after the sea had risen to its present level (Figure 32). This cutting back of the north end of the Cape was the first stage in the work of the waves. Soon, however, a good supply of sand and gravel was being brought westward by shore drifting from the marine scarp in the vicinity of The Highlands of Truro. Near Pilgrim Heights this sand began to form a narrow spit which grew steadily longer until it reached past what is now Pilgrim Lake, forming a protective barrier beach, preventing waves coming from the open Atlantic from attacking High Head. Between the new barrier and the old marine

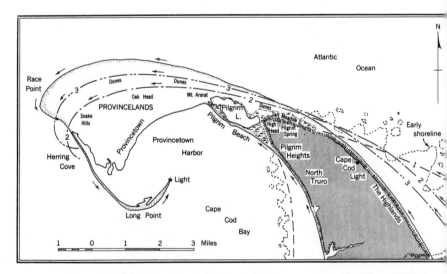

32. Growth of The Provincelands is shown in successive stages by shorelines labeled 1, 2, and 3. (Based on Davis' interpretation in "The Outline of Cape Cod," 1896.)

33. Salt Meadow, seen from the nature trail at Small's Swamp, Pilgrim Heights, Cape Cod National Seashore. In the foreground is the steeply descending slope of an ancient marine scarp, now covered by dense low shrubs. The flat ground of Salt Meadow is divided by a former tidal stream. Beyond are parabolic dunes that separate Salt Meadow from the open Atlantic Ocean.

ARTHUR N. STRAHLER

scarp of High Head there remained a narrow body of water—a *lagoon*. Today this water body has been narrowed by large sand dunes and the remaining part filled by tidal marsh deposits to form *Salt Meadow* (Figure 32). When you visit Pilgrim Spring, you can stand on the top of the old marine scarp and look across this tidal meadow to the dunes beyond (Figure 33).

As more and more sand was carried westward by shore drifting, the sandspit grew longer and developed a strong curve toward the southwest, so as to form the original Provincetown Harbor (Figure 32). We don't know exactly where this first sandspit was located, but it may have run along a line about through Mount Ararat, Oak Head, and the Snake Hills. It is difficult to locate the first sandspit because the area now has great sand dunes and these have buried the old sandspit.

As time passed the marine scarp of The Highlands of Truro was cut back still more, supplying more sand which moved west toward The Provincelands. Instead of following the line of the first sandspit, this material formed into new sandspits, each one lying farther north than the previous one. We can see the outlines of these sandspits as long, narrow sand ridges in the vicinity of the Provincetown Airport. They can be nicely viewed from the observation platform on the Race Point road. The final deposit is, of course, the present beach at Race Point lying between the Race Point Coast Guard Station and the Race Point Lighthouse.

But there is still more to the story of The Provincelands. Sand which reached Race Point did not all stop there. Much of it was moved southeastward by shore drifting from waves approaching from across Cape Cod Bay when winds blew from the west. This sand was moved past Herring Cove (where there is now a fine bathing beach) then out into the open water of Cape Cod Bay to form a sandspit curved strongly to the east and northeast. Today this recurved sandspit is called Long Point and ends at the Long Point Lighthouse. The Long Point sandspit forms a sheltering barrier for Provincetown Harbor, protecting it from waves that form when southerly winds blow across Cape Cod Bay.

PILGRIM LAKE

Finally, look at Pilgrim Beach and Pilgrim Lake. You can have a good close view of these features from the main highway leading into Provincetown. Pilgrim Beach is a narrow baymouth bar shutting off an ancient bay from the sea (Figure 32). This bay was formerly named East Harbor, but in 1869 the narrow inlet connecting it with the sea was closed to form Pilgrim Lake. Surface elevation of this lake is now about two feet above sea level. Where did the sand come from to form Pilgrim Beach? As we have already seen, a low marine scarp forms the western coast of Cape Cod in the area of North Truro. This scarp has been cut by waves of Cape Cod Bay when winds blow from the south and southwest. The sand removed from this scarp has been carried northwestward by shore drifting. It first formed a narrow sandspit lying off of Pilgrim Heights. The spit grew longer to the west until it reached the opposite side of the bay near Mayflower Heights, completely sealing off the bay and forming the present baymouth bar.

What the Tides Have Done

TIDES OF CAPE COD

Those of you whose first visit to Cape Cod was from a place far in the interior of the country may have been quite startled to see for the first time the tidal rise and fall of sea level. Perhaps when you arrived at the Cape the tide was high and the waves were breaking on the crest of the sand beach. Then, some six hours later, the sea had mysteriously drained away, exposing many tens of yards of mud flats beyond the beach (see Figure 39). Even those who have lived near the shore all their lives may have much to learn about the tides and the geologic work of the currents that are set in motion by tides.

A first step in understanding tides of Cape Cod is to study the manner in which the water level rises and falls. A simple way to do this would be to make a *tide staff* and attach it to the side of a wharf in a well-protected harbor, such as that in Provincetown (Figure 34). The tide staff is simply a long flat board which is marked off into units of feet, numbered from zero at the bottom to, say, fifteen feet at the top, like a large ruler. Now suppose that we have read the height of tide each half hour, noting the number of feet and half feet at which the water line is located. The observations are then plotted on a simple graph in which the height of tide in feet is numbered from bottom to top; the time in hours from left to right (Figure 35).

The tide graph shown here can illustrate correctly the tide at such ports on Cape Cod Bay as Plymouth, Barnstable, Wellfleet or Provincetown. Note that *high water,* which is the point of highest water level, occurred at about 1:00 A.M. and reached the 12-foot mark on the tide staff. Then the water level fell until about 6¼ hours later, at about 7:15 A.M., it had reached *low water* about on the 3-foot mark on the tide staff. This drop represents a tide *range* of 9 feet. The water then began to rise and 6¼ hours later again reached its high-water mark of 12 feet at about 1:30 P.M. The next low water, at 7:40 P.M., did not reach quite as low a point as the previous one. Now, we see that low water follows high water by 6¼ hours; the next high water follows by 6¼ hours. It is therefore obvious that one high water follows the previous high water by 12½ hours (12 hours 25 minutes). An explanation for this time schedule lies in the schedule of the moon, which the tide matches in length of time intervals.

34. A tide staff.

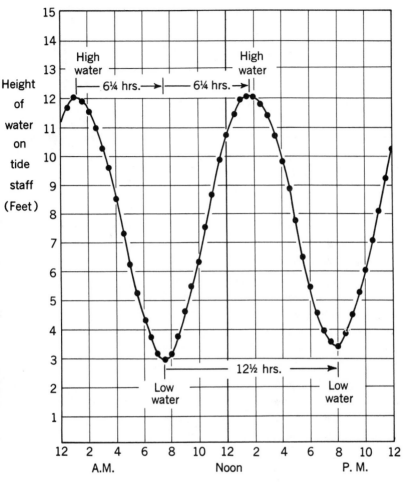

35. A tide curve for a typical day at a harbor on Cape Cod Bay. Each black dot represents a reading of the height of water. Readings are taken every half hour. (Based on data of Captain H. A. Marmer and the U. S. Coast and Geodetic Survey.)

There is not room in this small book to explain the cause of tidal rise and fall of water level. We shall simply have to note that the moon's gravitational attraction for the earth sets up the most important tide-making forces. True, the sun also sets up important tide-making forces, but the moon, being the closer of the two bodies, sets the time schedule for the tides. Now, the moon reaches its highest position in the sky every 24 hours and 50 minutes, which can be thought of as the *moon's day,* or *lunar day.* One high water is caused by the moon's being most directly overhead in the sky; the next high water by the moon's being directly opposite on the other side of the earth. Consequently there are two high waters in each lunar day and these occur 12 hours and 25 minutes apart.

Looking back at the tide curve which has been drawn for Cape Cod Bay, note that a black dot marks each half hour of time. The dots are close together near high and low waters, but are most widely spaced in the mid-tide periods between. This spacing of dots means that the water level changes only very slowly near high and low waters, but changes very rapidly in the mid-tide periods. Now you can understand why the tide seems to "stand still" near high and low water, but to fall or rise very rapidly in the mid-tide hours. In Cape Cod Bay, the water level changes at a rate of about two feet per hour in the mid-tide periods. No wonder you should take care to make for shore without delay as soon as the tidal rise begins, if you have been clamming far out on the mud flats at low water!

SPRING TIDES AND NEAP TIDES

If you have stayed at Cape Cod for two weeks or more, you may have noticed that at one time of the month high waters reached a higher level on the beach and low waters dropped lower than at another time of month. If you should compare your observations with the phases of the moon, you would discover that the greatest tide range occurs near the time when the moon is full and also when it is new. (By the word "range" is meant the difference in level between high and low water.) The range is somewhat less at times when the moon is in first quarter and third quarter.

The tides of greatest range, which accompany the phases of full moon and new moon, are called *spring tides;* those of least range, accompanying phases of first- and third-quarter moon, are called *neap tides.* Spring tides in Cape Cod Bay have an average range of ten to eleven feet; neap tides a range of around seven feet (Figure 36). If you are seriously interested in knowing exactly when high and low waters will occur on each day during your stay at the Cape, and how high and low these tides will be, you can purchase a book of tide tables from the U. S. Coast & Geodetic Survey for the price of one dollar. Of course, local newspapers will also give the information and you may also find it posted at your local beach headquarters.

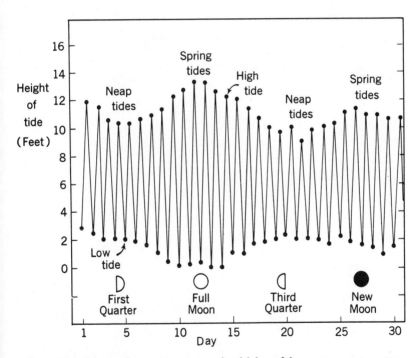

36. Dots on this graph represent successive high and low waters over a one-month period. Note how the range varies from spring tides to neap tides. The graph is a typical example for a harbor on Cape Cod Bay. (Based on data of Captain H. A. Marmer and the U. S. Coast and Geodetic Survey.)

FLOOD AND EBB CURRENTS

To the geologist, tides are important because the rise and fall of water level sets in motion alternate landward and seaward flows of water in the entrances to bays and harbors, and in tidal streams. Such water movements are called tidal currents (Figure 37). As tide level rises, a landward flow of water, the *flood current,* is

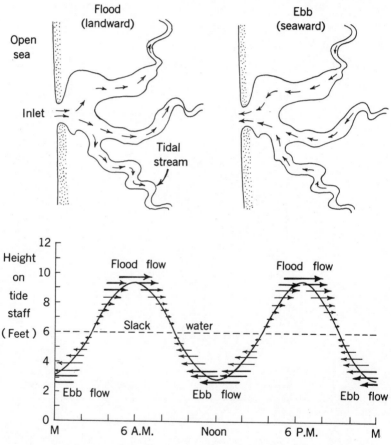

37. Flood and ebb currents in tidal streams are illustrated by sketch maps (above). A tide curve (below) uses arrows to suggest the direction and strength of the currents.

set up; this usually continues strong until well after the water level has begun to fall. The current then comes to a standstill, the *slack water,* after which the flow sets in again, but in reverse, to become the *ebb current,* which moves the water back toward the open sea. The ebb current flows until well after low water, when it weakens and another slack water point is reached. So, about every six and a quarter hours there is a current opposite to the direction of the previous flow.

Flood and ebb currents can be quite swift—three to five knots or more in the narrow entrances to certain bays and harbors, and in narrow tidal streams. Such speeds are capable of scouring the bottom and dragging along sand and pebbles. Where such scour has taken place, the bottom appears to have been molded into low ridges and troughs, known as *current ripple-marks* (Figure 38).

38. Great sand ripples produced by ebb tide currents on the floor of the Avon River estuary in Nova Scotia. Direction of the current is indicated by the arrow. Current ripples similar to these form on Cape Cod in favorable locations, such as in tidal inlets.

DEPARTMENT OF MINES AND TECHNICAL SURVEY, OTTAWA

Scour by tidal currents keeps the entrances to bays and harbors from being sealed across by sand carried along the coast by shore drifting. Without such tidal currents there would be few natural openings to the bays of a coastline such as that of Cape Cod.

MUD FLATS AND SALT MARSHES

Also of great importance to the geologist is the fact that ebb and flood currents can carry very fine material consisting of particles

39. Mud flats at low tide, Provincetown Harbor.

of clay and fine silt. At such times the water may be murky, or *turbid*, in appearance. The tiny particles are said to be held in *suspension*. Clay and fine silt can enter tidal currents from two possible sources. One is from streams that enter the ocean, carrying the clay and silt that was taken up by land erosion. On Cape Cod there are few flowing streams capable of carrying much sediment, so we must look to some other source. This second source is from the action of storm waves undermining scarps in which clay and silt layers of glacial till are exposed or disturbing glacial clay deposits in shallow water near shore. Once taken up into suspension,

ARTHUR N. STRAHLER

the clay and silt travels in longshore currents to be swept into the mouths of bays by the flood tide current. At slack water this sediment sinks to the bottom, forming thin layers of mud. Once deposited, the particles cling rather tightly to the bottom and are not easily dislodged. As a result, layer upon layer of mud accumulates, building up the floor of the bay and making the water shallower. Eelgrass, growing on the bottom, helps to trap sediment.

Finally the mud is built up close to the average sea level and becomes a *mud flat,* exposed at low water but covered at high water (Figure 39). A further development then takes place. Upon the mud flat there grow in abundance salt-loving plants, especially a kind of grass known as *Spartina*. The stems of these plants act as traps for more clay and silt, which is deposited at high tide until the surface is built up to the level of average high water. Such a flat surface is known as a *salt marsh* (Figure 40). It is laced through with narrow, winding *tidal streams,* or *tidal creeks,* which carry in the flood waters and return the ebb waters.

Cape Cod has many areas of salt marsh scattered along its coast-

40. A sinuous tidal creek meanders through salt marsh at Rock Harbor, Orleans, Massachusetts.   HAROLD L. R. COOPER, CAPE COD PHOTOS

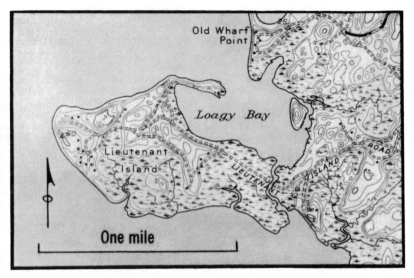

41. Salt marsh is shown on a topographic map by short horizontal lines and tufts of grass. This is a portion of the Wellfleet, Massachusetts, Quadrangle of the U. S. Geological Survey. The area is located in Wellfleet Harbor.

lines. On the Cape Cod topographic maps published by the United States Geological Survey, salt marsh is shown by a blue pattern of horizontally ruled lines over which are drawn little tufts of grass, symbolizing the salt marsh vegetation (Figure 41). One good example of salt marsh is the floor of the Pamet River, extending across Cape Cod at Truro. Another larger example is the salt marsh of Nauset Harbor, which lies landward of the sand barrier of Nauset Beach.

As a general rule, salt marsh has been formed and is presently forming landward of any baymouth bar or barrier beach which has enclosed a lagoon of quiet water, protected from storm waves. The largest such area of salt marsh on Cape Cod is about four miles long by two miles wide, and is known as The Great Marshes. This area lies west of Barnstable Harbor, separated from Cape Cod Bay by Sandy Neck, which is a broad barrier beach built by eastward shore-drifting. The accompanying map shows the principal salt marsh areas of Cape Cod (Figure 42).

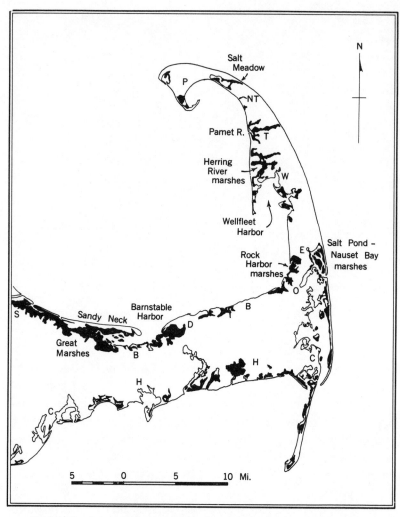

N

Salt
Meadow

P

NT

Pamet R.

T

Herring
River
marshes

W

Wellfleet
Harbor

Rock
Harbor
marshes

E

Salt Pond –
Nauset Bay
marshes

O

B

Barnstable
Harbor

D

Sandy Neck

S

Great
Marshes

B

H

C

H

C

5   0   5   10 Mi.

42. Principal salt marshes of Cape Cod are shown in solid black. (Based on maps of the U. S. Geological Survey.)

Some areas of salt marsh on Cape Cod have been put to man's use. First the marsh is *diked,* which means that a low earth wall, or *dike,* is built across the seaward end of the marsh, permanently shutting out the inflow of tidal currents. A network of long, straight ditches is then cut into the marsh, allowing good drainage of salt water out of the marsh through gates in the dike. Gradually fresh water replaces the salt, and a fresh-water marsh results. Under these conditions meadows are developed from which hay can be harvested. A good example of a diked and drained salt marsh is Salt Meadow, lying north of Pilgrim Spring. Large systems of drainage ditches can be seen in the salt marsh of Chase Garden Creek, between Yarmouth Port and Dennis.

The Pamet River salt marsh, mentioned earlier, was diked at Truro, cutting off the eastern half of the marsh from tidal inflow and converting it into a fresh-water marsh.

Ponds and Bogs of Cape Cod

FRESH-WATER PONDS

Much of the pleasant variety in Cape Cod scenery results from the presence of many inland lakes, ponds, and bogs, which occupy ice-block hollows or kettles in the outwash plains and moraines. Take for example the fine group of ponds east and northeast of Wellfleet, within the Cape Cod National Seashore (Figure 43). The largest of these is Gull Pond, next in size come Great Pond, Long Pond, Higgins Pond, and Slough Pond. One feature that is most striking about these ponds as they are seen from the air, or on the Geological Survey's topographic maps, is their roundness.

Were these ponds as round as this in outline when they were first formed, when the ice blocks that occupied them had just melted away? Evidently not. When first formed the outlines were much more irregular. The action of small waves easily undermined the loose sand and gravel of the steep sides of the kettles. Shore drifting moved the sand away from the steep scarps, building spit-bars across the small bays. In this way Great Pond became rounded and was separated by baymouth bars from Northeast

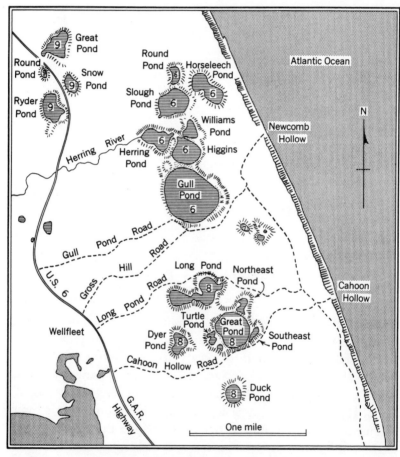

43. Sketch map of ponds of the Wellfleet area, Cape Cod. A numeral in the pond gives the water elevation in feet above mean sea level. (Based on Wellfleet Quadrangle, U. S. Geological Survey.)

Pond, Southeast Pond, and Turtle Pond, which were originally its bays (Figure 43). In a similar way Gull Pond was separated by a sand bar from Higgins Pond, and Higgins Pond in turn from Williams Pond.

WATER BELOW GROUND

Water levels in the fresh ponds of Cape Cod stand at elevations of from six to thirty-two feet above sea level. The geologist calls such ponds *water-table ponds*. To understand what this means, we must learn something about the subject of *ground water,* which is the term applied to water filling all open spaces between rock particles below the earth's surface. Cape Cod, being mostly a vast deposit of sand and gravel, can be thought of as a huge sponge. The hard mineral grains of sand and gravel do not fit very well together, so that when dry there is considerable amount of air space which cannot be closed up. When water is added, it displaces the air and can move easily, though slowly, through the sand and gravel under the force of gravity.

Therefore, when heavy rains and melting snows supply water to the ground surface, the water easily percolates through the soil, passing downward into the underlying material. Within a certain distance, which may be from a few feet to many tens of feet (depending upon the location), the downward percolating water comes to a level below which all of the pore spaces are already filled with water. This level is the *water table*. Below the water table lies the *ground water zone* (Figure 44). Here no air space remains unfilled and the water can move only very, very sluggishly under the force of gravity. The best way to find the water table is to dig or drill a vertical hole or well. If the well is deep enough, it will penetrate the water table. Then water will stand in the bottom of the well, rising to a given height and no higher. The level of water in the well represents the water table at that place. If many such wells are drilled, it will be found that the water table is not a horizontal surface (like a lake) but has higher and lower places, like low hills and valleys. In fact, the hills of the water table are usually located directly below the hills of the ground surface; the lower places of the water table are below valleys. Ground water moves very gradually from the higher to the lower levels.

Now, any permanent pond, lake, or stream, in a humid climate such as Cape Cod enjoys, is actually a place where the water table appears at the surface. The ponds of Cape Cod can be thought of as flat pieces of the water table, exposed to the air (Figure 44). From the shore of each pond the water table rises in a low slope away from the pond to low "hilltops" of the water table under the higher hill summits of the land.

FRESH WATER MEETS SALT WATER

What happens to the water table at the shoreline of the ocean? It slopes gradually downward to the average level of the sea. What happens when the fresh water of the land meets the salt water of the ocean? Fresh water is less dense than salt water and the two kinds of water do not mix very well. If we could cut a great vertical slice across a peninsula, such as Cape Cod, and see where the fresh ground water and salt ground water meet, we would find that they meet on a surface that starts near the shoreline in shallow water, slopes deeply downward toward the land, passes under the peninsula, then slopes up again to emerge on the opposite side in a similar manner (Figure 45). Altogether, then, the fresh ground water looks in cross section like a lens of a magnifying glass cut across; but the lower surface of the lens is much more strongly convex than the upper. The fresh ground water, being the lighter, is actually floating upon the salt ground water, just as a ship's hull floats by displacing the water around it.

The fresh ground water will extend down below sea level about forty times deeper than the height of the water table rises above sea level. For example, the water table in the vicinity of the rounded lakes near Wellfleet is about eight feet above sea level, judging from the elevation of the water level in the lakes, so that fresh ground water extends down to about three hundred and twenty feet below sea level. The lens of fresh ground water is main-

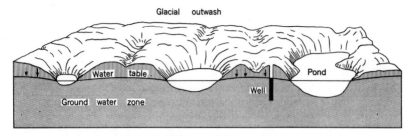

44. This block diagram of fresh-water ponds in glacial outwash shows how pond level is related to the water table.

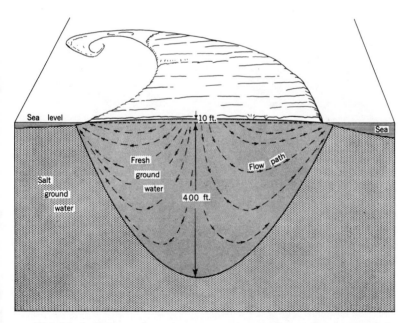

45. This block diagram shows in a very exaggerated way the extent of the body of fresh ground water beneath a sandy peninsula, such as Cape Cod. (The vertical scale is about forty times as large as the horizontal scale.)

tained by fresh water percolating down from the surface during the fall, winter, and spring in times of heavy rains and the melting of snow and ground ice. The fresh ground water moves slowly downward and seaward, finally escaping into the sea by seeping out from the shallow ocean bottom in springs.

THE CRANBERRY BOGS

As visitors know from travels about Cape Cod, the floors of many of the ice-block kettles contain cranberry bogs, rather than ponds of open water (Figure 46). On the Geological Survey's maps of the Cape, cranberry bogs are outlined by a solid blue line, in-

46. Two cranberry bogs seen from the air. These are beside Governor Prence Road, Eastham, Massachusetts. The straight, dark lines are drainage ditches. A forest of pitch pine surrounds the bogs.

HAROLD L. R. COOPER, CAPE COD PHOTOS

side of which are crisscross blue lines, representing ditches (Figure 47). Chains of cranberry bogs have also been developed along the floors of outwash channels along the south side of Cape Cod. Many of the cranberry bogs were developed on the flat, swampy floors of kettles which, since they were formed by the melting ice, were shallow ponds occupied by water-loving plants. Gradually the partly decomposed vegetative matter replaced the water surface, producing a bog across the entire floor of the kettle. The vegetative matter was compacted into a brown material known as *peat*, which was taken from the bogs by local people in the late 1700s through the early 1800s for use as fuel. The peat ashes were used as a fertilizer on fields.

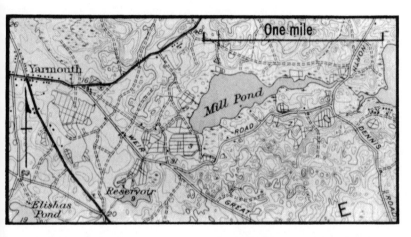

47. The rectangular line patterns on this map indicate cranberry bogs. Portion of the Dennis Quadrangle, U. S. Geological Survey, showing an area near Yarmouth.

What the Winds Have Done

DUNES OF THE PROVINCELANDS

All visitors to Cape Cod know about the sand dunes of the Provincetown area, because these dunes have been subjects for artists and writers for many decades. To the geologist a *dune* is any hill of loose sand brought to that place and shaped by the wind. There are, of course, many varieties of sand dunes the world over, but we are interested here in a class known as *coastal dunes*. Almost all of the world's sandy beaches are bordered by coastal dunes, built of sand blown landward from the dry surfaces of berms. On Cape Cod the most important dune belts border the beaches of The Provincelands, Monomoy Island, and Sandy Neck of Barnstable Harbor (Figure 48).

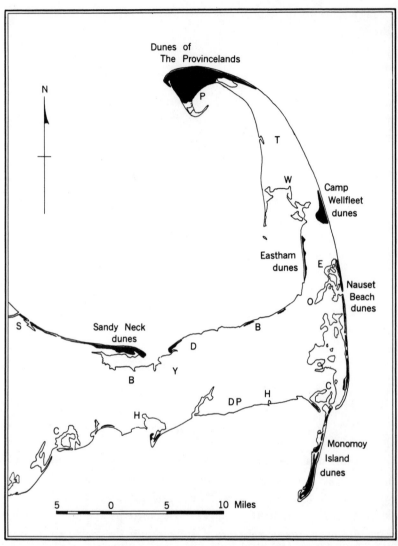

Dunes of
The Provincelands

N

Camp
Wellfleet
dunes

T

W

P

Eastham
dunes

E

Nauset
Beach
dunes

O

Sandy Neck
dunes

S

B

D

B

Y

H

DP

C

H

C

Monomoy
Island
dunes

5   0   5   10 Miles

48. The principal areas of sand dunes on Cape Cod are shown here in solid
black. (Based on the author's interpretation of maps by the U. S. Geological
Survey.)

Because of their great beauty and accessibility, the dunes of The Provincelands make the best area for dune study on the Cape (Figure 49). You will get a good first view of these dunes from the old marine scarp at High Head, or near Pilgrim Spring, where you can look across Salt Meadow to the dune belt. As you travel farther west along Highway 6 passing Pilgrim Lake, you will see on your right the steep slopes of dunes being built southward into the north shore of Pilgrim Lake (see Figure 52). The highway then cuts straight into the dunes. For the next four miles or so—clear out to the Race Point Coast Guard Station—dunes will be seen on all sides. Of course, many of the older dunes are now covered with a

49. Sand dunes of the Mount Ararat area of The Provincelands near Provincetown, Cape Cod, seen from the air. The view is southward, with Provincetown Harbor in the distance. Because the wind carries sand in a direction away from the observer, the visible dune slopes are smoothly rounded. Steep slip faces are hidden from view.   HAROLD L. R. COOPER, CAPE COD PHOTOS

forest of pitch pine and other plants, and it is only near the shore that the dunes are largely bare. A fine place from which to survey the dunes is the Pilgrim Monument in Provincetown.

PARABOLIC DUNES

Dunes of The Provincelands belong to a variety of coastal dune called by geologists *parabolic dunes*. In geometry the word "parabola" describes a form of line that appears to be bent into a beautifully shaped bow. A parabolic dune is a ridge of sand curved into this parabolic form, as seen from above or on a map (Figure 50). Imagine a bow and arrow, the bow drawn back ready to shoot and bent strongly into a parabola. The arrow now symbolizes the direc-

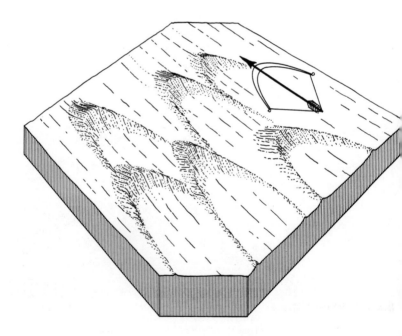

50. A bird's-eye view of a group of parabolic sand dunes. The arrow in the drawn bow indicates the prevailing wind direction with respect to the dunes. Length of the arrow is about one-half mile.

tion in which the wind blows to produce the dune, and is also the direction in which the sand travels and the dune as a whole advances. The highest points on the dune are found on the strongly bent part of the parabolic curve. In either direction from this summit area the dune ridge becomes lower and narrower, tapering down to the ends of the bow. Within the curve of the ridge is a rather flat, open sand floor, which is sometimes in the form of a shallow basin or depression (Figure 51). From this depression sand has been removed by wind, a process called *deflation,* and carried up to the dune crest. Because of this wind-blown depression the parabolic dune is sometimes also called a *blowout dune.* Sand which is carried over the dune crest falls upon a steep lee slope, which is very smooth and straight and has an angle of about thirty-four degrees measured from the horizontal. This clean, smooth

51. The inside of a parabolic sand dune, looking eastward toward the dune apex. The blowout area is in the foreground. This dune can easily be reached by a short walk from the Pilgrim Spring locality of the Cape Cod National Seashore.   ARTHUR N. STRAHLER

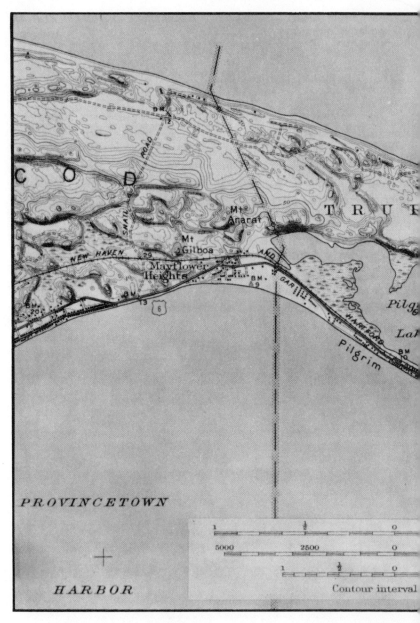

52. Dunes of The Provincelands, Cape Cod, show up clearly on this map published by the U. S. Geological Survey. Some shading has been added to the dune slopes. (Portions of Provincetown and North Truro Quadrangles.)

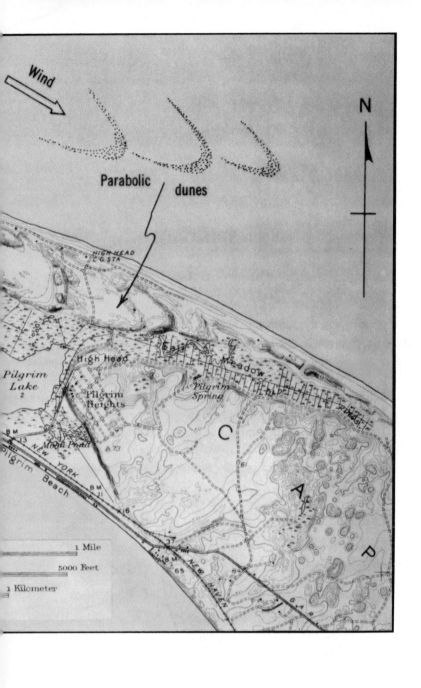

slope is called the *slip face* of a dune. As the slip face advances, it may encroach upon a forest, killing the trees, whose bare trunks and branches protrude grotesquely through the sand. The parabolic dunes also advance landward over salt marsh and we can see an example of this at Salt Meadow, near Pilgrim Spring (Figure 33).

If the pattern of the parabolic dunes of The Provincelands is examined, using the rule of the bow and arrow, it is seen that the prevailing winds which have formed these dunes blow from the northwest, which is not at right angles to the shoreline but instead rather obliquely to the shoreline. The dunes run in belts, and it is supposed that each belt has been formed from the sand of a former beach. As we have already learned, The Provincelands area was built of a succession of beaches, each one representing a re-curved spit-bar pointed west.

The highest points on The Provincelands dunes are along the older dune belts. Mount Ararat, for example, is over one hundred feet in elevation (Figure 52) and many dune summits west of it rise to over eighty feet. Town Hill, a dune summit on which the Pilgrim Monument now stands, was also over one hundred feet in elevation. Between the old dune ridges lie several ponds (such as Shank Painter Pond, Clapps Pond, Great Pond, and Grassy Pond) with water surface elevations of three to four feet above sea level. These are fresh water ponds occupying the blowout depressions between dune crests.

As one travels south, along the eastern coast of Cape Cod, coastal

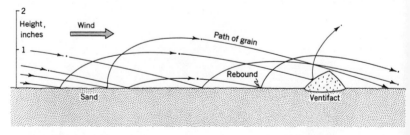

53. The leaping of sand grains impelled by wind is shown here in a cross-sectional diagram.

dunes are encountered in a narrow belt on Nauset Beach, and in several low dune ridges on Monomoy Island (Figure 48). These coastal dunes are only from ten to thirty feet in elevation and are irregular in form, in contrast to the high, well-developed parabolic dunes of The Provincelands. Low irregular coastal dunes are also found at various points along the Cape Cod Bay shoreline, those of Sandy Neck near Barnstable being the most extensive.

LEAPING SAND GRAINS

How is sand carried by wind? The grains move so fast that the human eye cannot see them in flight. But the process has been studied in laboratories where high-speed photographs show the paths of the grains. Each sand grain makes a long, low leap downwind, strikes the surface and rebounds like a little golf ball, repeating these leaps over and over again. This leaping motion is called *saltation* (Figure 53). Most of the leaps are very low—less than an inch or two off the sand surface, so that the moving sand can be seen as a filmy sheet which swirls about our ankles on days when the sand surface is dry and a strong wind is blowing. As grains strike the sand surface the forces of their impacts move nearby grains, causing them to be pushed a short distance downwind. So, in addition to saltation, sand on dunes moves by a slow creeping process, called simply *surface creep*. Sand which is carried by saltation over the crest of a dune may fall into a zone of quiet air and can move no farther. When enough of this sand accumulates in the lee of a dune crest, it can no longer remain at rest, but begins to roll and slide downhill. The process results in the formation of a smooth, steep slip face, which has already been described.

SAND DUNES AND CONSERVATION

Coastal dunes are strongly influenced by a very remarkable beach grass which can thrive and extend itself on a bare sand surface (Figure 54). The stems of this grass tend to check the wind

54. Beach grass on dune slopes bordering the beach of The Provincelands, just north of Pilgrim Heights. Sand carried inland (left) from the barren berm (right) lodges among the grass stems and builds the dune ridge into a substantial barrier.   ARTHUR N. STRAHLER

flow and make saltation of sand less effective. The result is that dune sand accumulates, building up the surface which is covered by grass. The effect of the grass is to hold the sand in dunes close to the beach and to cause them to be built up to higher levels than otherwise. The dunes thus come to form a substantial barrier which prevents the swash of great storm waves from sweeping far inland.

It is important to assure that the grass cover on coastal dunes is not killed off or otherwise destroyed by vehicles or construction, for the sand of an unprotected dune will be quickly carried landward and a deep depression (a blowout) will be formed close to the beach. Storm swash can then easily enter the depression to undermine slopes far back from the beach.

Provincetown relies upon the forest cover of the older dune belts

55. Successive ridges of dune sand run from left to right across this view, which is taken from the Race Point observation platform in The Provincelands. The nearer ridges have a forest cover of pitch pine, but the distant dunes, close to the beach, are largely bare of plant cover or have a patchy cover of beach grass. ARTHUR N. STRAHLER

to prevent the dune sand from moving southwest into the town and harbor. There was originally a good scrub forest cover here, but the early settlers carelessly cut the trees away, allowing the sand to begin to move toward the harbor. Then, between 1810 and 1830 beach grass and pitch pine were planted to stabilize the dunes. The forest is protected by law and will shield Provincetown against future encroachment by the dunes, although the bare dune ridges close to the north shore will continue to shift southward (Figure 55).

VENTIFACTS

Beaches have not been the only source for dunes on Cape Cod. The flat surfaces of the glacial outwash plain have been swept by strong winds since the time they were first formed. In places low dunes have been built of sand from the outwash plain surface. One zone where such dunes can be seen is just back of the marine scarp between Highland Light and Nauset Light. As the sand was removed from outwash plain surfaces, the pebbles and boulders remained behind, forming a surface covering known as *lag gravel*. Exposed surfaces of these pebbles were cut away and polished by the driving sand, so that today one can find wind-carved pebbles, called *ventifacts* by geologists (Figure 56).

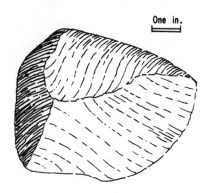

56. Sketch of a wind-faceted pebble found on Nantucket Island. (From a photograph by Edward Wigglesworth.)

Soils of Cape Cod

If you are particularly observant you will notice as you drive about on Cape Cod highways that in many places the upper few inches of the sandy soil is a very pale gray, almost white, whereas the sand below it is yellowish or reddish (Figure 57). This light-colored layer has been *leached,* which is to say that the coloring matter (which may be the dark brown humus from plant matter, or the reddish iron-oxide, rust, from decay of minerals) has been carried down from this layer by rainwater percolating through the soil.

The light-colored leached band forms a continuous layer below the surface of the ground, and is said to be a *soil horizon.* Above the light-colored horizon is found a thin dark layer, the A_0 *horizon,* which consists of humus and the abundant roots of plants. The uppermost dark mineral horizon is called by soil scientists the A_1

57. A podzol soil profile buried beneath a cover of more recent wind-deposited silt and sand. This exposure is in the wall of a gully at The Highlands in North Truro. The true soil profile begins near the base of the darker layer (top of the dark glasses). The dark glasses span the leached, ashen A_2 horizon. Beneath this is the reddish B horizon. ARTHUR N. STRAHLER

horizon; the light-colored leached layer is called the A_2 *horizon.* Below this lies the reddish *B horizon.* The entire soil is called a *podzol,* which in the Russian language means "ash-soil" (Figure 58). The pale gray A_2 horizon does in fact seem to resemble the color of wood ashes. We have borrowed the Russian term because much of our early scientific knowledge of soils was first developed by Russian scientists.

Podzol soils are found over vast areas of the forest lands of arctic Canada and Siberia. A cold, wet climate is required for the development of podzol soils, but where the soil is formed on sand, as on Cape Cod or other sandy coastal belts of our east coast, podzol develops in climates which are less severe. The reason is that leaching of the A_2 horizon takes place much more rapidly in sand than in clay soils.

The podzol formed on sand areas is particularly favorable for the growth of certain species of pines and oaks. These trees are small and stunted, for the soil is not rich in nutrients and holds little water between rains. The fallen needles of the pine trees, as they decompose, produce weak natural acids, which cause the leaching of the A_2 horizon. Thus soil and forest go hand-in-hand; each influences the other.

Not all of the soil of Cape Cod is podzol, of course. In many places the leached A_2 horizon is not seen and instead an upper layer of brown, humus-rich soil rests upon the reddish, iron-stained sand and gravel.

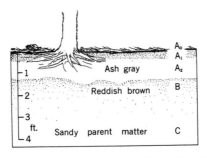

58. The horizons of a typical podzol soil on Cape Cod. Compare with the photograph of this soil, Figure 57.

The Geologic Future of Cape Cod

We have seen how the ice sheets laid down the basic material of Cape Cod, and how the work of waves, shore drifting, tidal currents, and winds have changed the outline of the Cape, removing parts of it and building new parts. These geologic processes of removing and adding are going on today and will continue to act for thousands of years to come. The outer coast of the Cape will continue to be cut away, narrowing the forearm of the Cape and perhaps even cutting it entirely through. The Cape will grow ever longer by the addition of beach deposits and dunes accumulating in The Provincelands and on Monomoy Point. Changes on the inner shoreline of Cape Cod Bay and on the shore of Nantucket Sound will be much slower and less spectacular because of the smaller size of storm waves. Here the engineering works of man can prevent much of the erosion and entrap the sand that moves by shore drifting.

Cape Cod is indeed a wonderfully varied place for the study of geology and the processes that develop a landscape. Far from being just a simple sandy peninsula, the Cape is a mosaic of many kinds of patches of ground, each different in origin from the patch next to it, but all fitted together by a single history of growth and change.

For those who take their geology very seriously and want to learn more about the details, there is on page 109 a list of books, reports, and articles which geologists have written about Cape Cod. Some of these reports are difficult reading for those who have not studied geology, but all have passages written in a clear and straightforward style that will mean a lot to any serious reader. Those who take geology seriously also want accurate, detailed maps which show topography as well as man-made features. For this purpose topographic maps of the U. S. Geological Survey are available at small cost. An outline map on page 98 gives the names of the individual map quadrangles and shows the areas they cover. By all means have a set of these maps with you when you visit the National Seashore or vacation on Cape Cod. Plan your trips to places of geological interest and follow the route closely on these maps. These fine maps show every hill and valley by means of contour lines and will enable you to estimate your elevation at any point.

Topographic Maps of Cape Cod

Detailed, large-scale topographic maps of Cape Cod, Marthas Vineyard, and Nantucket Island are available to the public through the United States Geological Survey. The maps are on a scale of 1:24,000 (one inch=2000 feet) and take the form of rectangular sheets, known as *quadrangles*. A single quadrangle covers seven and a half minutes of latitude and longitude, although a few are irregular in size to accommodate extensions of land beyond the usual quadrangle limits. Each quadrangle is designated by a name. The accompanying index map shows the names and locations of quadrangles.

Topographic maps are printed in five colors. Cultural features, such as roads, railroads, cities, towns, and civil boundaries, as well as lettering, are in black; water features are in blue; and the features of relief, such as hills and valleys, are shown by brown con-

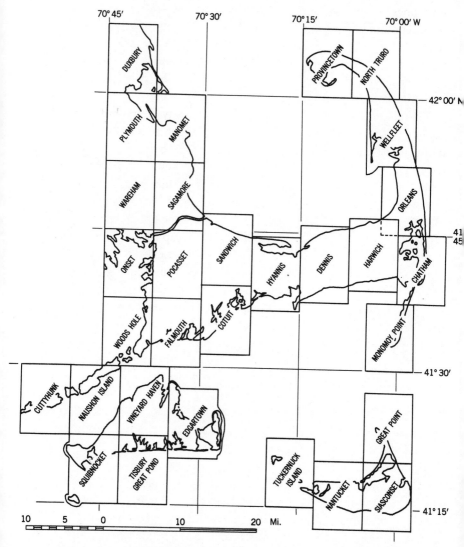

Index map showing the names and locations of U. S. Geological Survey 7½-minute quadrangles of Cape Cod, Marthas Vineyard, and Nantucket.

tour lines. Cape Cod quadrangle maps on the scale of 1:24,000 use a contour interval of ten feet. Many hill summits, ponds, and road intersections are labeled with the surface elevation to the nearest foot. Areas of dense vegetation, such as forest or woodland, are overprinted in a solid green color. Finally, the principal roads and highways are shown in red.

The price of a single topographic map is fifty cents, but a discount of twenty percent is allowed on orders of twenty dollars or more. Prepayment is required and may be made by money order or check, payable to the "U. S. Geological Survey." Cash may be sent in the exact amount at the owner's risk, but postage stamps are not accepted in payment. Orders should be addressed to Washington Distribution Section, U. S. Geological Survey, Washington 25, D.C. Simply designate the desired map by its quadrangle name, state, and scale; e.g. "Orleans, Mass., 1:24,000." Shipments of approximately six maps or less are folded and mailed in envelopes, unless unfolded copies are requested in the original order. Larger quantities of maps are rolled and forwarded in tubes. You may obtain free of charge an information circular and index to topographic maps of the state of Massachusetts by writing to Map Information Office, U. S. Geological Survey, Washington 25, D.C. A sheet explaining the symbols used on topographic maps will accompany the circular.

APPENDIX II

Cape Cod's Climate

Cape Cod, along with mainland New England and the other states
of the northeastern United States, has a *humid continental climate*
characterized by a moderate to large annual range of temperatures
and well-developed winter and summer seasons. Precipitation is
ample in all months and favors the development of forests as the
natural vegetation. Cape Cod, however, also illustrates the *marine,*
or *maritime,* influence through its closeness to the great water body
of the North Atlantic. Although prevailing winds are westerlies and
tend to bring climate extremes of the North American continent
to Cape Cod, the ocean water serves to ameliorate the climate
somewhat, reducing the extremes of summer heat and winter cold,
as compared to places inland in southern New England.

The graph on the next page gives Cape Cod's climate statistics
on temperature and precipitation, as recorded by the U. S. Weather

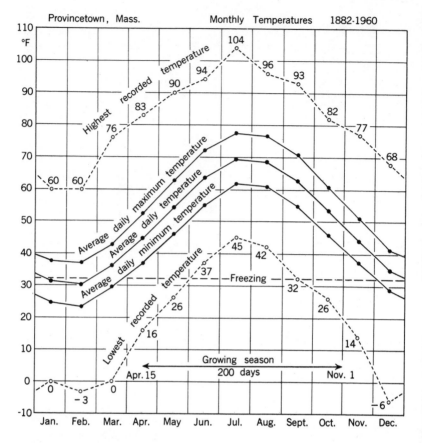

Provincetown, Mass.   Monthly Temperatures   1882-1960

Highest recorded temperature

60 60 76 83 90 94 104 96 93 82 77 68

Average daily maximum temperature

Average daily temperature

Average daily minimum temperature

Freezing

Lowest recorded temperature

0 -3 0 16 26 37 45 42 32 26 14 -6

Growing season
200 days
Apr. 15   Nov. 1

Jan. Feb. Mar. Apr. May Jun. Jul. Aug. Sept. Oct. Nov. Dec.

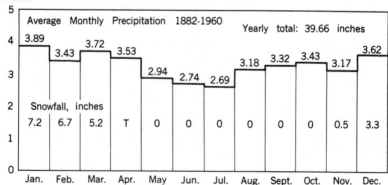

Inches

Average Monthly Precipitation 1882-1960   Yearly total: 39.66 inches

3.89 3.43 3.72 3.53 2.94 2.74 2.69 3.18 3.32 3.43 3.17 3.62

Snowfall, inches

7.2 6.7 5.2 T 0 0 0 0 0 0 0.5 3.3

Jan. Feb. Mar. Apr. May Jun. Jul. Aug. Sept. Oct. Nov. Dec.

Bureau at Provincetown over a span of sixty-seven years of observations (during the period 1882–1960). Of course, there are other climate elements that this graph does not show; namely, relative humidity, cloud cover, fogs, and the direction and speed of winds. The three temperature curves formed by the dots and solid lines are averages of almost sixty years of records. For the visitor and resident of the Cape, the two curves of greatest importance are those labeled Average Daily Maximum and Average Daily Minimum. The first of these is obtained by averaging the highest thermometer readings of each day for the entire month, then averaging those averages for the entire period of record. The second curve similarly averages the lowest readings of each day. For example, in July the highs average 77.5°; the lows average 61.6°. The average daily range in July is thus 15.9°. Although individual days will have highs and lows quite different from the averages, the figures give you a pretty good idea of what to expect. Compared with Massachusetts mainland stations, the average daily temperatures in July and August are not much different on Cape Cod than at, say, Blue Hill (near Boston) or Worcester, but are appreciably lower than within the city of Boston. However, the July average daily maximum temperature is from two to three degrees lower on the Cape than at inland stations, reflecting the cooling effect of summer afternoon sea breezes. One also finds that the January and February average daily temperatures on Cape Cod are several degrees warmer than at inland stations in Massachusetts. Thus the ocean serves as a reservoir of warmth in winter.

It is interesting to find that the coldest month on Cape Cod is February, whereas at inland locations January is the coldest month. The delay in reaching the annual low point is explained by the fact that large water bodies cool more slowly than land areas. Both

Monthly temperature and precipitation averages for Provincetown, Massachusetts, based on observations in the period 1882 to 1960. (Information is missing for a number of years in this period.) Source: U. S. Department of Commerce, Weather Bureau, Climatography of the United States, No. 86-23, *Climatic Summary of the United States,* Supplement for 1951–60, New England. Washington, D.C., 1964.

January and February average below freezing on Cape Cod. On the average, one hundred and five days per year register temperatures below thirty-two degrees. The average date of the last killing frost in spring is April 15; the first in the fall is November 1. These dates give an average growing season of two hundred days, which is considerably longer than for places inland in southern New England.

Total yearly precipitation on Cape Cod averages almost forty inches (39.66 in.) and is fairly evenly distributed throughout the months of the year. The bar graph on the opposite page gives the details. One can see a definite precipitation maximum during the winter months, along with a tendency to lower amounts in the late spring and early summer months. Altogether, much more rain and snow falls on Cape Cod than is returned to the atmosphere by evaporation and by transpiration of plants. Consequently, a good water surplus exists and is responsible for maintaining the level of the ground water table in fresh-water ponds.

During the winter, Cape Cod is visited by severe coastal storms whose centers pass to the east and south of the Cape. At such times northeast winds blow, giving the *nor'easter,* which is so distinctively a part of New England's climatic pattern. Low clouds, a steady driving rain or drizzle, and bone-chilling dampness characterize the nor'easter.

Fogs are relatively frequent and dense on the Cape. Fog results from the passage of warm or mild, moist air over cold waters of the Labrador current, which makes its way southward off Cape Cod. The moist air is chilled by loss of heat to the cold water surface and easily reaches the point of condensation, producing the fog droplets. Thunderstorms of the summer are not as common over the Cape as over the mainland, because the cool water surface tends to reduce formation of the strong vertical air movements required in the growth of thunderstorms.

APPENDIX III

The Cape Cod National Seashore*

In accordance with its stated purpose, "to conserve the scenic, scientific, and historic heritage of the United States for the benefit and enjoyment of its people," our National Park Service administers the Cape Cod National Seashore, a unit authorized by act of the United States Congress on August 7, 1961. Until recently, Cape Cod's natural and historic scene was preserved by the good taste and care of individuals, the towns, and the commonwealth of Massachusetts. The establishment of the Cape Cod National Seashore now more permanently assures this protection. Wild beach, heath, forest, and ponds are no longer threatened here in one of the last expanses of uninterrupted natural lands along the

---

* This account is based on, and includes excerpts from, brochures of the United States Department of the Interior, National Park Service.

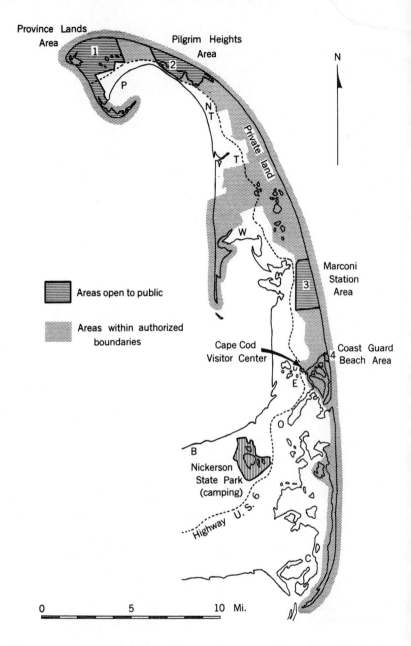

Map of outer Cape Cod showing the boundaries of the Cape Cod National Seashore and public areas in 1966. Based on a map of the National Park Service, U. S. Department of the Interior.

Atlantic. The Seashore will ultimately embrace some twenty-seven thousand acres of land and promises to keep intact the charm and beauty of the Old Cape for future generations.

The accompanying map shows the extent of the Cape Cod National Seashore. Two classes of areas are distinguished: areas open to the public; areas within the authorized Seashore boundaries but presently consisting of privately owned land. More than half of the land of the Seashore is private property. Owners may keep their homes, hand them down to their children, or sell to others.

Public use areas within the Cape Cod National Seashore are four in number. Northernmost is the Province Lands Area, including the Race Point and Herring Cove beaches and a large area of dunes and ponds. Here the National Park Service provides guarded beaches, guided walks, and interpretive panels. Second is the Pilgrim Heights Area, consisting of seventeen hundred acres. Here we find an interpretive shelter and picnic area. Two trails of scientific and historic interest are developed. These are the Pilgrim Spring Trail and the Small's Swamp Trail, on which both guided and self-guided walks may be taken. Particularly noteworthy are a pitch pine upland forest, bearberry heath-covered slopes leading into a large glacial kettle, and azalea-blueberry vegetation on the kettle floor. There are good views of Salt Meadow and the coastal dunes; access on foot is provided to these features.

Third of the developed public areas is the Marconi Station Area, in which Seashore Headquarters are located. An interpretive shelter gives a description of the famed wireless transmitter by which Marconi sent the first transatlantic radio message on January 19, 1903. The high marine scarp and broad beach provide a spectacular hiking area. Guided and self-guided walks give access to White Cedar Swamp, a rare vegetation type. Fourth is the Coast Guard Beach Area, at the head of Nauset Bay and Nauset Beach. Here, on Great Beach, guarded swimming and surf fishing are provided. A guided walk into the Nauset Marsh is given in summer months.

The Cape Cod Visitor Center is the first point of call for those arriving at the Seashore. This Center, which houses a fine museum and auditorium, is located in Eastham, close to Highway 6 and overlooking Salt Pond. Here one can obtain information on lectures and tours, and study the museum exhibits which deal with geology, anthropology, natural history, early exploration, and settlement of the outer Cape. Afternoon programs at the Visitor Center feature slide talks or movies of subjects related to the National Park Service and other conservation organizations. A series of evening lectures is also held here, or in good weather, in an open amphitheater nearby. All educational activities available to the visitor are described in the Summer Interpretive Program, given out at the Visitor Center. Public use areas will change year by year as more land is acquired within the authorized Seashore boundaries. New interpretive shelters and trails are being developed.

An independent organization, the Massachusetts Audubon Society, maintains the Wellfleet Bay Wildlife Sanctuary, entered from Highway 6 just north of Wellfleet. Here one finds nature trails, displays, and other facilities within an area of 325 acres including pine forest, moor, and marshland. The Society also provides to the public its Beachbuggy Wildlife Tours. These are nature tours taken in specially equipped vehicles, know locally as *beachbuggies,* capable of traveling through the loose dune sands. One two-hour tour is scheduled at high tide and takes the visitor to Nauset Beach where many shorebirds can be seen. An all-day tour covers the Great Beach (Nauset Beach) within the National Seashore. A longer tour, taking the entire day, is to Monomoy National Wildlife Refuge. Transportation is by boat to the island, then by beachbuggy. Schedules of tours, reservation information, and prices may be obtained by writing to the Wellfleet Bay Wildlife Sanctuary, Box 236, South Wellfleet, Massachusetts.

Nickerson State Park, situated two miles southwest of Orleans, offers wooded camp sites grouped about several kettle ponds. The entrance to this park is on Highway 6A between East Brewster and Orleans.

A List of Selected Books and Articles for Serious Study

"The Outline of Cape Cod" by William M. Davis, American Academy of Arts and Sciences, Proceedings, vol. 31, pages 303–332, 1896. This article is now available in *Geographical Essays* by William M. Davis, edited by Douglas W. Johnson, Dover Publications, Inc., New York, 1954, pages 690–724. Professor Davis discusses the erosion of Cape Cod by waves and the building of The Provincelands.

"Geology of the Cape Cod District" by Nathaniel S. Shaler, U. S. Geological Survey, Eighteenth Annual Report, Part 2, pages 497–593, 1898. Although a much older report than that by Woodworth and Wigglesworth, Shaler's work has much of value to offer.

Geography and Geology of the Region Including Cape Cod, the Elizabeth Islands, Nantucket, Marthas Vineyard, No Mans Land and Block Island by Jay B. Woodworth and Edward Wigglesworth, Memoirs of the Museum of Comparative Zoology at Harvard College, vol. 52, 322 pages, 38 plates, Cambridge, Massachusetts, 1934. This comprehensive volume is the best of the older general works on Cape Cod geology but may not be readily available except in large city and university libraries.

"Pleistocene Geology of Western Cape Cod, Massachusetts" by Kirtley F. Mather, Richard P. Goldthwait, and Lincoln R. Thiesmeyer, Geological Society of America Bulletin, vol. 53, pages 1127–1174, 1942. This report has detailed maps of the glacial deposits of western Cape Cod. Particularly interesting are the many fine photographs of ventifacts, of which more than two thousand were found.

"Glacial Geology in the Buzzards Bay Region and Western Cape Cod" by Kirtley F. Mather, Field Trip No. 4, *Guidebook for Field Trips in New England,* Geological Society of America, New York, 1952.

"Pleistocene Geology of Outer Cape Cod, Massachusetts" by John M. Zeigler, Sherwood D. Tuttle, Herman J. Tasha, and Graham S. Giese, Geological Society of America Bulletin, vol. 75, pages 705–714, 1964. This study is concentrated upon the age and origin of the glacial materials of the eastern Cape, with particular attention to the sediments exposed in the outer marine scarp beween Nauset and The Highlands.

These Fragile Outposts—A Geological Look at Cape Cod, Marthas Vineyard, and Nantucket by Barbara Blau Chamberlain, The Natural History Press, Garden City, New York, 1964, 327 pages. Authoritative and written in fine literary style, this comprehensive volume covers not only all phases of Cape Cod geology, but tells much about the local history of environmental change and economic development since the earliest settlement of the Cape. Unquestionably the best single reference work available to the serious student of Cape Cod geology and related fields of natural history.

INDEX

Place names mentioned as examples of particular geologic features are indexed with the feature in parentheses following the place name.

Arthur N. Strahler, Professor of Geomorphology at Columbia University, received his B.A. degree from the College of Wooster in 1938 and his M.A. (1940) and Ph.D. (1944) in Geology from Columbia, where he was successively appointed Britton Scholar and University Fellow. For the past twenty-five years Dr. Strahler has led a distinguished teaching career at Columbia. He was chairman of the Department of Geology from 1959 to 1962.

He is author of more than thirty articles in professional and technical journals. His college textbooks on physical geography (*Physical Geography,* John Wiley & Sons, revised 1960; *Introduction to Physical Geography,* John Wiley & Sons, 1965) and geology (*The Earth Sciences,* Harper & Row, 1963) are widely used throughout the United States and Canada, and in many other countries of the world. He is currently preparing a junior high earth science text for Harper & Row.

Dr. Strahler has had a long-standing interest in the Wisconsin ice sheet and has made detailed field examinations and maps of its glacial deposits in localities ranging from Wisconsin, across Ohio, New Jersey, and New York, and as far northeast as central Maine. These studies have included analysis of the glacial deposits of Cape Cod and Long Island. He has also been interested in coastal geomorphology and shoreline processes, including dune development, and has conducted studies along the Atlantic coast for the Office of Naval Research, Geography Branch.